# Let My People Go Again

## *By Raymond Bush*

*"Oh what can I do, or what can I say whether by the dark of night or the light of day, there is simply not enough time in this life to express the joy in my heart when I consider how lovely thou art, alas I know I will make this Valentine's Day wish the cover of my book so that the whole world may look and be as I am…"Amazed". Happy Valentine's Day Phae." ~ Ray Bush 2/14/11*

ISBN Number: 978-0-6151-7583-6

Contact Information:
Raymond Bush
30799 Pinetree Rd
PMB 251
Pepper Pike, OH 44124
Email: raybbush@hotmail.com

## *An introduction to a preface to a revision*

To take a second look, to reconsider, to revisit, to make more clear, to further expound upon, to subject to further scrutiny, to view from a different place in time…

I had not thought to make a revision on this book until after I wrote the revision, yet these were the thoughts and ideas that came to mind as I began to write this preface, which is really a continuation of a subject and topic that should be near and dear to all of our hearts—all 6.5 billion of us. The subject that we all have skin invested in the game and the one that we all instinctively play to win, you guessed it, the game of life! Yet for time's sake, I'm primarily concerned with the 30 million or so that dwell in America, after decades of experience and plain old trial and error and error and error…

These are my thoughts. Let me know if you can relate. Life is the medium where the spiritual and physical realms meet. Life can only move in one direction. Life is reciprocal—you take out what you put in (plus interest)—even if that something is nothing. In this realm life and time are inseparable and they are not stagnating. They won't stand still for you to figure out which way is up. This life is all we have to express all that we are, for better or worse, for richer or poorer, in sickness or in health, until death does us part. Dare I say in a sense we are all married to life. I dare and I do! I have yet to meet the man or woman who intentionally had a desire for a life of misery, pain, failure, and poverty, or would you want a marriage like that? I hope not!

There are three dynamics to life which just so happen to coincide and complement each other, and there are also three dynamics to America. The 'life' dynamics (extremes) are positivism, rightness, and forward momentum. The American dynamics are life, liberty, and the pursuit of happiness. I know America's not perfect but she strives to do what's right and make amends when she doesn't, but to always keep the nation moving forward. We are, as America is, a works in progress. According to the laws of physics, for every action there is an opposite and equal reaction. Based on this logic, there has to be dynamics of death: negativity, leftness, and backward momentum. The coinciding American sentiments are death, slavery, and the pursuit of misery. These are the two roads/paths/recipes—one to success and the other to failure. The only cycle more vicious than a Harley Davidson is the one Leftists build when they try to solve the problems they create. If you don't mind having your intelligence insulted and being detached from reality, then go Left young man, go Left. Beverly Hills and a ghetto both have this in common—they lived in the minds before they lived in the lives of the people that live there. Everyone is indeed entitled to their own opinion, yet the course and nature of life is above them all. It's called the truth. If God/life had not intended for men and women to move forward through life, then we would all sit on our faces and talk with our "cans." No matter how much the leaders on the left would like to make it so, lies can't replace truth.

The fundamentals, the basics, the core, the root, the base, the foundations are at the start of every endeavor or activity. From the building of a house, a business, a sports dynasty, a relationship, a movement, or a nation, it is imperative to start out on the "right" foot with a solid foundation. How else would you expect it to stand or last if it's not built on the truth? It stands to reason that a life needs to have a base of truth to be successful. The nemesis code graphic is a visual illustration of the eternal perpetual battle between moving forward versus backward, up vs. down, based on our thoughts, words, ideas, actions, feelings, reactions, and willpower. Time plus direction plus percentage of momentum will determine the potential productivity of your life be it positive or negative. The nemesis (adversary) code is essentially asking the question, are you friend or foe to yourself, family, friends, nation, life or God? In regards to life and to relationships, can two honestly walk together unless they are in agreement?

There is beauty in a marriage between a man and a woman, especially in America when they incorporate the dynamics of life and America in the form of being supportive, forgiving, generous, understanding, protective, hardworking, honest, trustworthy, and faithful—you may need to sound and fire proof the bedroom! Since I published in 2007, the battle for America has accelerated and intensified exponentially. We are on the brink of having people take more life from life than people placing more life into life. Life and reality are one and the same. Successful life explodes into reality. Failed life implodes into reality. Bottom line, some people want you to stay still (not grow) and others want you to grow and live and reach your true potential, which are important not only for you and your family and friends, but America is also hanging in the balance. If you happen to be blessed with children and you teach to love and embrace life, then you have already succeeded at being a parent. The rest is up to your kids.

So let me be clear in this revision. If you don't know whose house is bigger, the White House or God's House, or you don't know spiritual forward from spiritual backward, and up from down, you could be your own worst enemy. There is a three house rule: #1 God's House, #2 Your House, #3 White House. If you don't know politics, you may very well vote to enslave yourself and not even know it. How then would you know the beginning of evil is to turn your spiritual back on life? Are we clear?

There is a Dead Sea of corruption in D.C., and it is about to flood our nation with a tidal wave of poverty, crime, violence and death. Either we can build a spiritual dam to stop it or America will drown in perdition.

Maoist leftism ~ Anarchist progressivism ~ Fascism ~ Marxism ~ Card check ~ Cash-4-clunkers Communism ~ Liberalism ~ Socialism ~ Deception ~ Bribes ~ Bailouts ~ Stimulus package ~ Cap-n-trade Uni-healthcare ~ ACORN ~ NAACP ~ La Raza ~ NEA ~ Apollo Project ~ Lies ~ Theft ~ Fraud ~ Greed Deceit ~ Kings ~ Queens ~ Czars ~ Tyrants ~ Dictators ~ Racist ~ Bigots ~ Elitist ~ Sexist ~ SEIU ~ AFL-CIO ~ UAW

The Leftists have finally hit the spiritual wall (backbone) of America; will it hold?

| Faith | Valor | Love² | Moms | Truth² | 9-12ers | Honesty | Tea Parties | Hope |
| Sacrifice | WRWL | Ernie | Dale | Jesse-Lee | Rush | Quinn + Rose | Glenn |
| Cara | Honor | Ray | Sara | John | Mark | Shawn | Matt |
| Liberty | Empathy | Joy | Fox News | Peace | Jesus |
| C O U R A G E x z |
| You * |

City: _____
State: _____

Conservative (up)
N
Dems (Left, Backward)  W←+→E  Republicans (Right, Forward)
S
Liberal (down)

* All in all, you can be a "real" brick in this wall, why?
Because it's about "dam" time for a real change in D.C.!

5

# A Baker's Dilemma

## *(a slice of life)*

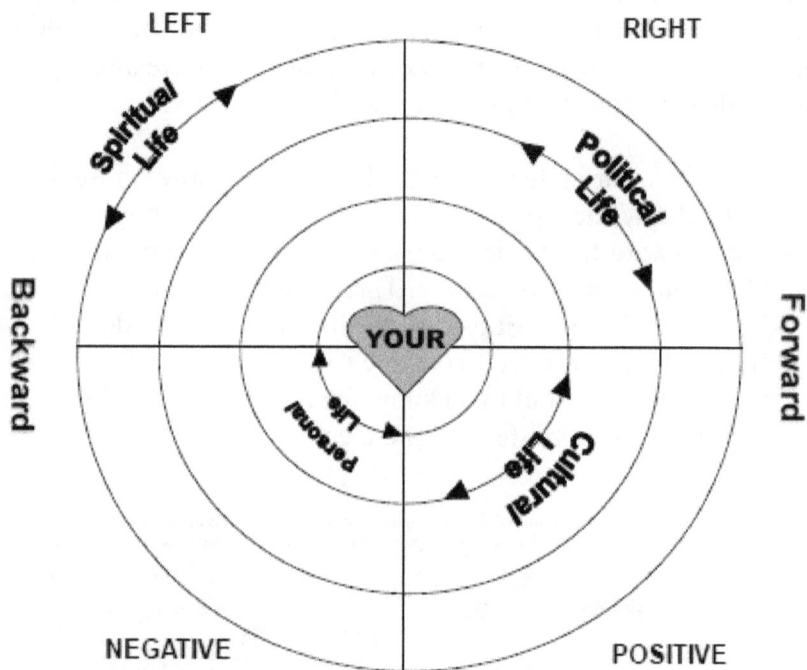

LEFT                 RIGHT

Spiritual Life

Political Life

Backward

YOUR

Forward

Personal Life

Cultural Life

NEGATIVE            POSITIVE

How can you hope to have a whole life (person) whether it be cake or pie, if you can't determine which direction (recipe) is based in the truth or a lie (e.g. angel-food, devil-food, red velvet, lemon cake, apple, cherry, pumpkin or sweet potato pie?

# The Ascension and the Vortex

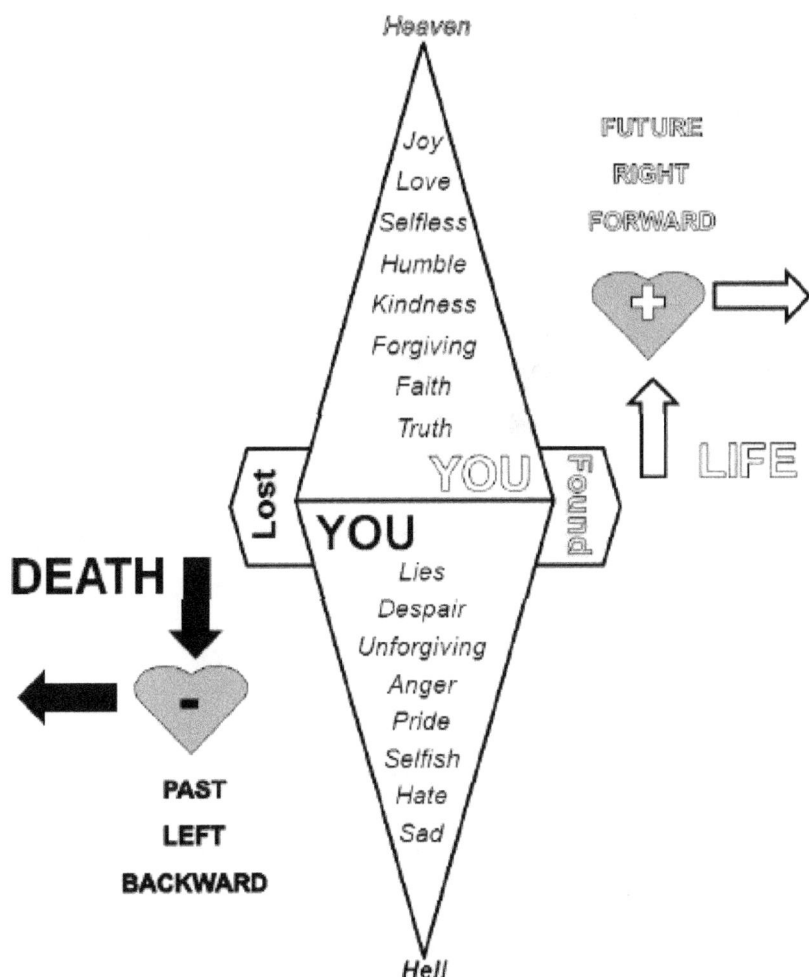

Heaven

Joy
Love
Selfless
Humble
Kindness
Forgiving
Faith
Truth

YOU

Lost

**YOU**

FUTURE
RIGHT
FORWARD

LIFE

**DEATH**

**PAST**

**LEFT**

**BACKWARD**

Found

Lies
Despair
Unforgiving
Anger
Pride
Selfish
Hate
Sad

Hell

Which YOU are **YOU** becoming?

The 3 circles: Life, Time, and Man.
Time and Life move to the "right",
Whereas Man is the only creation that
God has given the power to choose his direction.

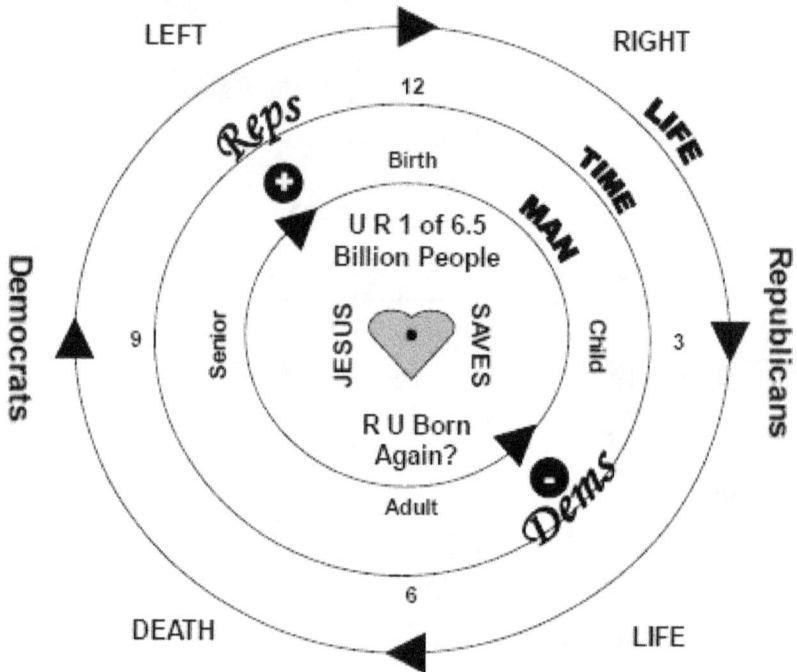

Why kick against the goads, or forces, or life?
Why live a lie? You will only be hurting yourself in the end.

## QUOTES AND SUCH

Since life and reality are one and the same, if you detach from one then you detach from the other: ergo if you want to live in the "real world" where your life is taken seriously then move with life to the right, and if you want to live in a fantasy/sub-reality where your life is not taken seriously then move to the left. It's your choice.

In life with all of the many things worth living for, certainly and ironically there is one thing above all worth dying for—life.

R. Bush's first two laws of invariability: *Nature abhors a vacuum* 1.) Concerning the mind, if the light is on then the room is not dark, and if the room (mind) is dark then the light is not on, in which case if the dark (blind) lead the blind they will both fall into a ditch. 2.) Concerning motion, if you're not moving forward in life then you are moving backwards or at best you are standing still. In either case you are still being left behind. See Matthew 12:30.

A great servant makes a good leader and a good leader makes a great servant.

The key to the equation (mystery) of life, time and man is synchronicity. Expressed mathematically: You + Time + Direction x % = Legacy = Destiny/Fate. Forward $\rightarrow$, Backward $\leftarrow$, Up, Down, Time/Speed x Fast/Slow x Positive/Negative x Intensity/Momentum. Once in Christ, you simultaneously move forward and up as you leave self behind. Then the variables of % of intensity, determination, time and speed will determine Positive vs. Negative legacy, which will determine destiny or fate. Those that thirst and hunger for righteousness will be filled. Oneness with Christ is oneness with life is oneness with God.

Life Bomb – when a person is loaded, packed, strapped, and down with love, light, life, truth, joy, peace and courage then intentionally walks into the dead darkness of Leftism…Boom!!

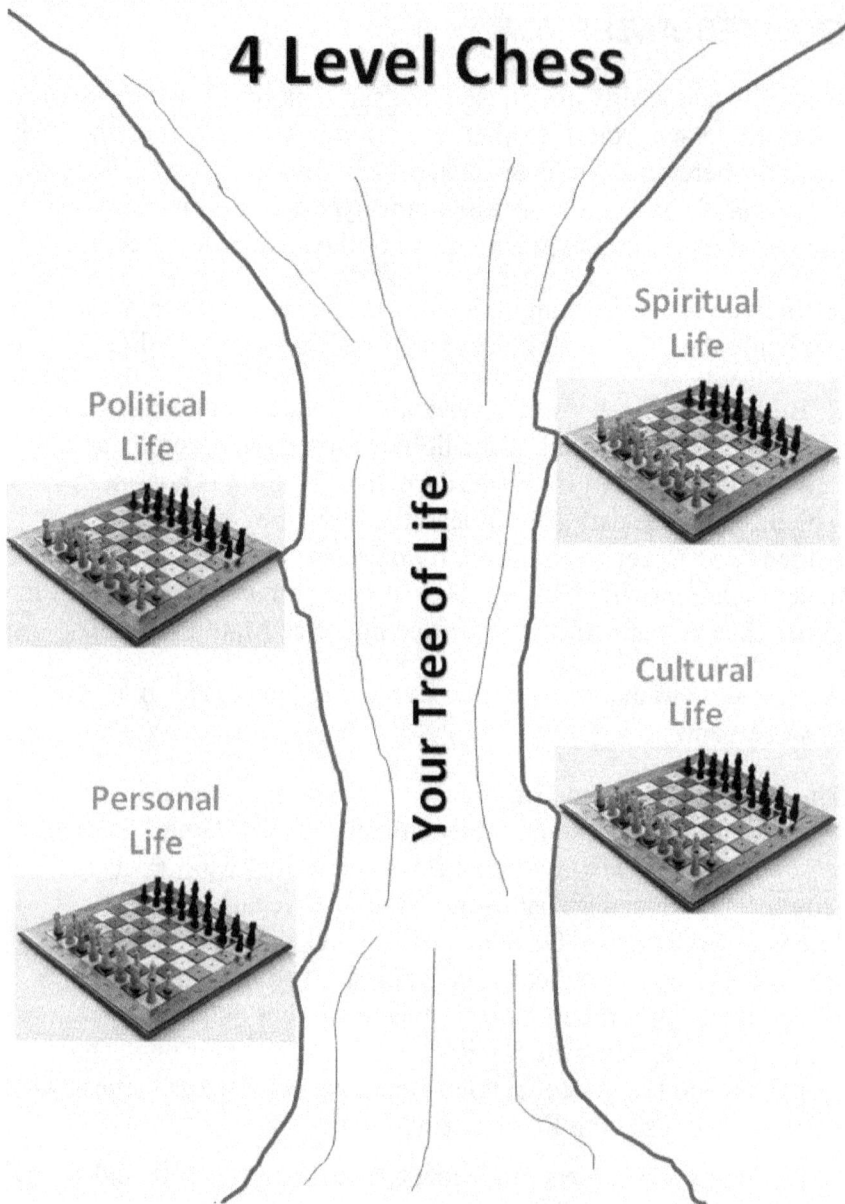

# 4 Level Chess

Spiritual
Life

Political
Life

Your Tree of Life

Cultural
Life

Personal
Life

## LIFE

Life! What is it? Where is it? Who has it? How do you get more of it? How are you treating it? How is life treating you? Is it really possible to be larger than life? If life is for the living then what about the dying? Life on the one hand can be at times wonderful, exciting and just plain fun, and then on the other hand, the one that nobody likes, it can be cruel, painful and bitter. Yes life really can be bitter sweet. And yes life has two extremes. Fortunately for us here in America we have the freedom and the right to choose so much as it is in our ability to do so. Life…it's more than a breakfast cereal. You feed your family life. It's much more than a board game you play with friends. Indeed it's more than a prison sentence given to some people who break the law. Wouldn't it be good to have life and have it more abundantly? Life is always, always, always on (ready) yet the question is are we ready to live and is there any difference between living and just going through the motions? What can we say about life? Life is spiritual (spirit) in that you can only experience it through your senses—sight, sound, smell, taste and hearing. In fact, life is a spiritually-generated, interactive, ambivalent construct. In other words, since man is a spiritual being, life is what we make of it. Life is cyclical (circular) in that you catch what you send, you reap what you sow, and what goes around comes around. Also, we (like life) are both moving. We are not getting any younger you know.

Dare I say that your #1 relationship in life is your relationship with life. I dare because you are in life and life is in you. Your experiences in life are largely determined by your outlook on life. Question is, do you want the most or the least out of life because there are three dynamics (extremes) of life—right, forward, and positive. Also conversely the opposite of life obviously is death which also has three extremes—left, backwards, and negative. If you look at your life from a philosophical, chronological, and spiritual perspective the rest of your life is to the right of your present position, i.e. your future is moving forward and to the left is your past and it's dead because you can't change it. There is absolutely no sense (nonsense) in looking let alone moving in a direction that life's not going. This is called common sense.

Life is more than fame, fortune, power and good looks. There are people with those things and they are still empty and miserable. It is possible to succeed in business/career and/or higher education and still be a failure at life overall. The key to a successful life is to take your whole life seriously and do the same to everyone in your circle and that you meet (just remember you can lead a horse to living water but you can't make them drink). The clean little secret about life is that if you don't agree with the direction of life you are already on the road to failure. Our thoughts, words, and ideas are spiritual as well they are the food, fuel, and energy that will propel your life down a path with life or against it. Your mind is the processing center or battleground between the physical and spiritual realm. Our actions and reactions are the confirmation codes between the good and bad.

The bottom line on this experience called life is that it always has and always will be moving to the right and the very contemplation to the contrary of this fact is where all hell broke loose in the human race. It's the place where the bible describes the fall of man i.e. the acquirement of the knowledge of good and evil. In this one act of rebellion against God, Adam and Eve created in themselves a world, a universe of lies and a world, a universe of truth. Life is sustained by truth not lies. This is the place where emotions, sentiments and feelings clash with reason, logic, and intellect. It's where fantasy slams into reality, pro-life meets pro-death ideology, down through the centuries even to this very day, hour, minute, and second. This is why there cannot be any compromise or bipartisanship between the left and right.

There is no common ground between truth and lies, life and death, light and dark have no relationship with each other. There is absolutely no way possible to have a honest, intelligent, mature, civilized conversation with a person who can't or won't accept the significance and relevance of keeping a good relationship with life in regards to your experiences in life. You may as well be speaking with a person who believes the earth is still flat (a "flat-earther") because of the cyclical nature of life people on the left who are detached and opposed to life are in effect at war with themselves, with each other, with time (killing time), life and God and not to mention they are on a collision course with the people moving in the right direction the people who have learned to treat life as good as they want to be treated by life. Yet on the other hand and further more the people who continue to look to government and material goods and turn their spiritual backs on God, life (reality) truth, the people that don't want to "fly right" continue to rebel the more society will spiral out of control the more people will become detached and destabilized from life, God and each other men women children born and unborn lives are smashed together and destroyed. Entire families, neighborhoods, cities, states and even countries are being pulled into spiritual darkness accompanied by the political religious cultural and business pimps who instigate, propagate and cultivate an atmosphere of victimization on the population the vortex will grow stronger and stronger.

The lies of the left are the primary reason that the inner cities are dying not only economically but emotionally and intellectually and culturally as well. All the while the poverty pimps continue to instigate and promote civil unrest in people who all ready have a disharmonious relationship with life. They blame people on the right or America or God instead of simply looking in the mirror. The truth is that life, like America, you & your computer, is "garbage in garbage out" or "good in good out." The fact is it is not the people on the right making life hard for them when it is life itself trying to discourage negative behavior and encourage good (right) behavior. It is not about their civil rights; it's about the "wrongs" that are causing all the grief. Unity in the truth brings peace, harmony, prosperity and security. Unity in lies brings war, disharmony, poverty, and violence. It is not safe or wise to invest your life (little life) in rubbing life (the big life) the wrong way since political, cultural and personal life all originate from the spiritual realm of the mind, so spiritual life is more important and takes priority over the rest.

Life is good but the world can be a cold cruel place there are people and spiritual forces who will gladly have your entire life for breakfast life a bowl of cereal they will play you and your family's life like a board game and when they are done with you, fold you up and put you away or even you yourself can make one wrong turn (left) and wind up with a life sentence behind bards or even the prison bars of a self=destructive lifestyle i.e. drugs, sex, alcohol, cigarettes, gambling, overeating, etc. To live life successfully it is imperative that you see the spiritual realm clearly and first. Like an optometrist helps you to see the physical world clearly, this "eye doctor" wants to help you see the spiritual world clearly as well.

The perfect yet devastating parallel between the physical and spiritual realm is the tragic catastrophe of the oil well spill down in the Gulf of Mexico. Even as it is clear to see that there is no way to put an actual price tag on the ecological and economic devastation to the region as millions of gallon of oil have spilled into the gulf in just a little over two months, and as this nightmare unfolds before our very eyes most Americans are completely blind to another spill that (dare I say) makes this one pale in comparison. I dare. The spiritual spill of lies into America, but primarily the inner cities, are hardest hit for some. Ten decades and trillions of 'gallons of lies' have been pouring into and saturating everything in sight. The devastation is catastrophic. The oily slickness of lies such as..."you can turn your spiritual back on the flow of life and still stay attached to reality"...or..."the government can meet your needs (nannystate) better than God or you can spend your way out of dept or you can take the life of an unborn baby and still keep a safe and civil society to name a few. The proverbial ecological destruction of the inner cities is breathtaking from the high crime, poverty, unemployment, drop out rate, teen pregnancy, unwed mothers, taxes, poor healthcare and diet, plus all the coping addictions. Like the birds of the Gulf covered in oil and unable to fly, so likewise these priceless "city birds" of all shapes, sizes and colors...mostly black, white and brown...all created in the image of God, all created with the ability to fly yet most of the young ones don't even know they were made to fly and the old ones' wings have atrophied and are too weak to fly. Some are too afraid, too lazy, some want a free ride and some hate to see others even try to fly and worst of all are the ones who flap around in the muck and mire and just pretend to fly. The devastation from the "Hell-Well

Lies" in terms of human capital is incalculable. Cap the well and the clean-up begins.

While the ability to cap the oil well in the Gulf was elusive at best for BP, all that's required to plug a spiritual well from Hell is for inner city people to stop believing lies. If we cap one city then the rest will follow suit. Eventually the secret to a successful, safe, low corporate tax rate, economically robust and thriving society is for the people to build and create an atmosphere of success with the brick and mortar of respect, responsibility and discipline along with sacrifice, hard work and perseverance. If you build it they will come!

**Political Life:** of leaders and followers and of mice and men. The problem that we have here in America, besides a failure to communicate, is a real life, real time rendition of a good politician (A.G.P.) vs. a bad politician (A.B.P.). Right after spiritual life is political life as the next in the line of power in America. We have two parties: one born in the truth, the other in a lie; two movements: one positive and the other negative. We have two directions: one forward and one backward; two agendas: one to enslave you and the other to liberate you. We have two ideologies: one righteous and the other unrighteous. We have two policies: one doomed to fail and the other bound to succeed; two timeframes: one party leans toward the future and the other the past. We have two end games: one success and the other failure. Now it doesn't take rocket scientists or theologians to figure out the guilty party.

The truth of the matter is, by the power of your vote you are as your movement is. In other words, if your movement was born out of a lie, then the only way for it to grow is it must be fed with a diet of deceit and deception. We know that everything based in a lie is doomed to fail because only the truth can stand the test of time. You don't have to see a person's life that's committed to crime to know it's not going to end well. It was a failure from the start. We know there are two sides to every story. Two sides to every coin. Two sides of the political aisle, yet if you can't understand "political speak" you will be deceived and made to be the "tail." You will be convinced that you should be grateful for being kept in a failed mindset.

We know that lies in a sane civilized world are worthless, yet in an insane, uncivilized world (nation) they are priceless. Unlikewise, truth in a sane civilized world is priceless, yet in an insane, uncivilized nation it is worthless. The question is, which America do you want to raise your family in? The lines of communication between leaders and followers have become really twisted in America. The voices of life, success, and freedom have their own place of residence with immovable, unchangeable addresses. Herein lies the key to understanding political speak. "A bad politician" (ABP) can't tell you about life, success, and freedom from an address of death, failure, and slavery. And a good politician (AGP) wouldn't waste time trying to deceive you.

The list of differences between AGP and ABP are like night and day. They really make the distinction between mice and men. For instance: AGP upholds the constitution plus first and second amendments, is strong on national defense and support of the troops, supports free market capitalism, small efficient government, and knows that the government works for the people. They believe first and foremost in the Judeo-Christian values. They raise the bar of morality. They strive to balance the budget and cut deficit spending, and also lower corporate and personal income taxes. They support police and fire departments. They would rather teach you to fish and are generally all around pro-life, liberty, family and American values. It's one thing to have a corrupt politician now and then, but it's a whole different ballgame to have a corrupt movement—a dead one. They both can't be right. ABP is the exact opposite of AGP. "Birds of a feather." The trick is they can't let you know the truth about the direction of their movement because who in their right mind would vote for their own demise, so they distract, accuse, vilify, blame, isolate and attack their opponents for the very same things that they are guilty of being—racists, sexists, bigots, homophobes, and elitist. Everything calls to its own, and the fruit does not far fall from the tree.

Their other trick is to neutralize, pacify, stagnate, cripple, and destroy the minds and will of their followers to be free and independent, but to be unforgiving and vengeful by taking and giving them other people's money or "free" food, housing, clothes, etc. This is how they can kill two birds with one stone and still appear to be paragons of virtue on the outside yet this is the darkness of deceit where mice pretend to be men and women. With leaders like this, a follower does not need an enemy...seriously. FYI to all the so-called moderates and independents, your positions do not exist in the spiritual realm. No man can be independent of both "kingdoms", right and left. No man can honestly belong to both parties at the same time. To straggle the fence is to be blind from knowing between night and day. "Be ye either hot or cold, cold or hot, but not lukewarm." You can't take a stand until you make a choice. You can't make a choice until you make up your mind. You won't make up your mind until you take your life seriously. Most people don't take life seriously until they are at the end of their rope or until it's too late. Will you?

**Cultural life:** is a combination, compilation, and collection of individuals and groups of people with countless thoughts, words, feelings, ideas, emotions, passions, and deeds with varying degrees and levels of actions and reactions which lead to a multitude of experiences and behaviors. Both good and bad are all acting, interacting, reacting, entangling, intertwining and colliding with each other. Plus when you consider the time factor that some events happen in a split second, some minutes, some hours, days, weeks, months, years, decades, centuries or millennia, all swirling around in a living collage, a mosaic, a work of art, a harmoniously, disharmonious symphony of life. Wow! Oh what a beautiful mess we are. Now with all that in mind, consider the American culture. We are a nation that has reached the pinnacle of societal evolution. We are the most technologically, modern and advanced country in the world's history, yet at the start I would like to give credit and honor where it is due. Thanks be to God and second to our armed forces. America is the most dynamic and the most diverse, most decent country in the world. We are the most free, liberated and open society. America is the most prosperous, generous and industrious nation in the world. We are the most righteous, sacrificing, and tolerant civilization in history to date. America wow! Obviously not all Americans see the country the same way. Essentially some see the glass (country) as half empty and some see it as half full. Dividing the nation are the Ameri-cans and Ameri-can'ts. The reason the line between the two has become so blurred is because of our three most time-consuming pastimes: work, education, and entertainment. In other words, as a nation we are what we do: work, learn, and play. In America there are more jobs, careers, industries, institutions, organizations, associations and unions, from medical to auto, to education, to real estate, to religion, to food, to retail, to music, to Hollywood, to construction, to sports, to outer space, to media, to manufacturing, to civil service, to political, to judicial, to administration, to banking, to litigation, to the multitude of entrepreneurs, from Wall Street to Main Street, from public sector to private sector, white collar to blue collar. I owe, I owe so it's off to work I go (author unknown). The bottom line of the matter from the political, to the cultural, to the personal, to the spiritual, we all fall into one of two extremes, either individually or collectively, we all lean left or right.

These are some of the extremes that manifest in America. Life is extreme, death is extreme, truth is extreme, and lies are extreme. Love is to hate as prosperity is to poverty, as righteousness is to unrighteousness, as legitimate is to illegitimate, as legal is to illegal, as freedom is to slavery, justice to injustice, reality to fantasy, intelligence to ignorance, educated to uneducated, optimism to pessimism, peace to violence, humility to pride, selfless to selfish, productive to lazy, forgiveness to unforgiveness, lawful to lawless, ethical to unethical, independence to dependence, normal to abnormal, mature to immature, competence to incompetence, priceless to worthless, civilized to uncivilized, and these are only a few extremes that shape America. I'm sure you can think of a lot more. The point is that truth and lies, morality and immorality, are opposite and offensive to each other. Spiritually they are intolerant of each other. We as human beings are but pawns in an eternal chess game of good and evil. The best deal is that we get to choose.

The dirty, filthy, disgusting, low-down secret about America is that the people on the side (path) of unrighteousness, immorality and lawlessness have secretly, covertly and stealthily high-jacked the path of righteousness, morality and lawfulness; they and their co-conspirators in the lame-stream media—the unions, litigation and judicial fields. So what's forward is backward, and what's backward is forward, what's up is down and vice versa. Due to political correctness, they falsely use our pro-American values and virtues against us. The people who don't tolerate the lies of intolerance are labeled intolerant and now they become the ones who can't be tolerated. Go figure. Case in point, every single American should ask themselves, "Am I my brother's keeper?" Going forward this question will become increasingly more relevant in the days ahead.

While it's true that the life you have within you (the little life) is all your own to do with as you please, in regard to this life (the big life) that we all share, if you develop a negative dysfunctional attitude (outlook) on life, as much as you may or may not hate to hear it, anyone who cares for you and this nation have a vested interest in your success. For at least two very good reasons, a nation is only as strong or weak as its citizens. If a growing number of Americans become dependent or employed by the federal government, the more the government will have to raise taxes on people and businesses to support their underlings and life-support victims. The point is America did not get to be the number one superpower in the world by being weak, dependent, insipid and cowardly. Ironically and hypocritically the Left vilify, attack and rod the very people they look to for life support economically. Even Fido knows not to bite the hand that feeds him. The people who want what's right for the nation to keep moving forward in a positive direction into the future are now guilty of being intolerant, mean, selfish, and evil, whereas the high-jackers are praised for being kind and benevolent. Now good is evil and evil is good. This has to be the largest and most devastating case of Stockholm Syndrome in modern history. America is in a nose dive about to slam into the ash heap of history. It may be too late to pull out of this tailspin. Now might be a good time to brace for impact ff you are not your brother's keeper. The second reason is more important than the first because as a Christian it is our job to turn as many people from dark to light, from lies to truth, from death to life, from slavery to freedom, from failure to victory, and to be clean, whole, free, and mature. This is the same battle that began over 2,000 years ago on Calvary's cross where the Lord paid the price for the sins of the world. This is the message of the gospel to repent, turn from sin, and be born again. There is still no greater love that a man has than to lay down his life for his fellow man. Are there any brother's keepers in the house?

"The Pop Quiz Game Show" – this one question is for all the chips, all the marbles, all the stakes, winner takes all. The question: between the two political parties, from which side does all the racism and bigotry in America originate? Answer: {pause} the Leftist, Socialist, Progressive, Liberal, Communist, Democratic Party. Correct!! {applause} Ding! Ding! Ding! Ding! Ding! Tell 'em what they've won Johnny! The prize: an all expenses paid golden opportunity to complete Dr. Martin Luther King's dream! {gasps} {applause} Thank you, thank you all, and good night everybody.

FYI – there are only two freedoms in this life, to either do what's right or to do what's wrong to progress or regress, to regenerate or degenerate, to move forward or backward, up or down, left or right.

**Personal Life:** "But seriously folks" is a line that a comedian might use when they want to distinguish between a joke and a serious matter. In your personal life have you ever had a person that you could look them in the eye and not take them seriously—essentially play that person for a joke? What's an even more intriguing question: has anyone that you know ever played you for a joke or even worse have you ever played yourself? As I mentioned in my preface, this life is all we have to express all that we are, for better or worse, for richer or poorer, in sickness or in health, until death does us part. Dare I say in a sense we are all married to life. I dare and I do! What is it that we can't do when we take ourselves seriously? Lose weight, get out of debt, finish school, get a job, stop smoking, drinking, drugging, gambling, etc. Have you ever seriously considered the potential havoc and devastation you can cause to yourself, family, friends, descendants, neighborhood, city, state, country, if you place your one precious life (trust) and future in the hands of political, religious, cultural, and business leaders who don't even take life seriously? Do you really think that they take you seriously…really?

Nevertheless, there is One who takes your life seriously. To Him you are no joke. To show His love He sent His son (John 3:16) to pay the price to give you the right to live a clean, free, whole, and mature life. Also this same One was on His throne, long before the universe and earth were made, and before America was born. He is the "Right." He is for the right, uprightness, and righteousness. The expanse of His domain is such that all success in life has to move in His direction including business, sports, education, relationships, and family. They all have to move forward and up (right) to have positive successful growth. Everything good comes from Him and returns to Him—love, truth, peace, joy, faith, etc. To the people on the political right, you may be on the path of righteousness but you don't own it until you reach the cross of Christ. You're still not safe to the people on the political left. The people on the right are the least of your concerns. All of your collected arms are still too weak and too short to box with God. This life is His creation and He is going to finish what He started, with or without your help, so unless you can redirect the course of life, stop time in its tracks, or go back and rearrange the past, why invest your life in a dead, failed, defeated movement (Leftism). Are you serious? Really? The truth is, to all men and women who wish to oppose life, truth, love, joy, peace, and freedom, when your time in this life is over you will not have to be bothered with being exposed to life ever again.

This is a special message to the future of America: young people, please, please, please slow down, slow down, slow down. You are all racing into spiritual darkness as if you had just won the lottery or American Idol. Here's a news flash, this just in, you are not a gangster, player, mack, "G", old "G", pimp, hustler, etc. You are a victim caught in a trap. It was socially engineered, politically constructed, and culturally maintained. It is a false fantasy/reality (sub-culture) with real life consequences designed to keep you weak, broke, angry, violent, afraid, incarcerated, or dead. The truth is the real "Gs" are certain politicians, religious and business leaders that are in control of your reality (life). If you have ever seen the movie "The Matrix" or better yet "Inception" more accurately describes how they implanted lies into the minds of your parents, grandparents, and great grandparents. Now three and four generations down you are the product (fruit) of those lies. God knows the abuse, neglect, lack of support and abandonment. He knows and He cares, but if you teach the lies to your kids they may never be able to wake up from the dream/nightmare. If you wish to wake up and rejoin reality…I'm going to count to three, snap my fingers, then you turn around, straighten up, and fly right. Ready…one…two…three…wake-up!

P.S. To all the Diva's out there, if you would spend as much time making the inside as attractive as the outside, then you would stop attracting so many zeros. Then maybe a hero (Mr. Right) might appear.

Conclusion: This is real soul food if you would eat and digest it. It is better for you than BBQ, ribs, chicken, burgers and dogs. The truth can make you clean, free, whole, and mature so you will be able to have life and have it more abundantly. Do the "Right" thing and get "Right" with God because who in their "Right" mind would oppose living life the "Right" way?

## The Big Deal about the Big Picture about the Big Choice about the Big Life (God)

"The Left" and "The Right" are two completely separate self-contained ideological life systems which are in fact arbitrary and vehemently opposed to one another. They each dwell in the hearts and minds of all humanity including the spiritual, political, cultural, and personal aspects of life. These obviously manifest in our business, educational, and entertainment endeavors, experiences, and behaviors each to its own.

Each system has its own set of principles, values, priorities, directions, agendas, objectives, goals and modes of operation. At the heart of the crisis in America and the world is system sustainability. The mental outlook on the right is in agreement with life, being attached to reality, truth, independent thought, morality, and God. This system can sustain itself with positive growth while on the other hand the system on the left is the antithesis of the right being attached to lies, fantasy, immorality, dependence and godlessness cannot sustain itself. Since leftism goes against the very "grain of life" it is indeed unsustainable. The only way for the system to survive and grow is for it to attach to the other for life support until the U.S. becomes a 3rd World nation. It will continue to feed and grow until it totally consumes the other system, yet like fictional vampires of Hollywood can't see their own reflection in a mirror, leftist can't or won't acknowledge that they are the very cause of the problem they claim to solve. They are indeed the reason America is on its way to "hell in a picnic basket."

These are indeed the most perilous times in American history. The people who believe in American "exceptionalism" not only have enemies outside the gate as well as inside the gates, and both adversaries are formidable together. They are all but unstoppable. To make matters worse the nation is bankrupt economically, morally, and spiritually. This is the big deal about the big picture. This is indeed a referendum on America and Americans. We have a big choice to make about the Big Life (God). Will we turn our collective spiritual backs on Him and embrace "The Little

Caesers" (government). An unintelligent electorate is America's worst liability, and the leftist's best friend and most useful idiot. It's sad to say, but what else can you conclude about people who vote for the demise of their country and themselves as well? Be that as it may, the Creator has made the creation to move and grow in a forward, right, and positive direction. Leftism is a crime against time, life, humanity, and God.

"The Big Life" has made us an offer we cannot refuse. If you choose not to take your "rightful" place in life, if you choose not to allow the spirit of life to dwell and flow through you, then all I can say is that's a big mistake because no matter how many, or what color, or race, or country or nationality, male or female, young or old, rich or poor, God is all inclusive and He is all exclusive even though He is full of mercy, grace, and compassion. For us yet He is not going to turn or stop the creation for one nanosecond because we don't want to live "right." If you detach yourself from life, you may get your wish forever. P.S. I wouldn't call his bluff if I were you.

In the end, no matter how religious, no matter how many traditions, and no matter how much we've been brainwashed, indoctrinated, or filled with self-pity, the battle will end where it began (the spiritual realm). In the end, the one who had the first say will have the final say. In the end everything returns to its own—eternal life to the living and eternal death to the dead. In the end, ending up on the lifeless side of life is really no way to live. Bon appetit my dear fellow American!

# FORWARD

This little book is dedicated to America. May the components of her flame (life, liberty and justice) endure the encroaching darkness only to rise and shine and burn brighter than ever, until we can all find our way out of inner and outer darkness. I think in a way since we are the "stuff" that America is made of, you might say this book is dedicated to you.

We Americans being at the pinnacle of societal evolution are deeply embedded in a quagmire of thoughts, feelings, ideas and desires. Which, if not resolved, will either tear the nation apart and drive it over a precipice into backward darkness ruled by civilized savagery, or she will inevitably become whole (for the most part) so that her light may burn brighter than ever for us and the whole world to see. At the core of the dispute seems to be Black vs. White, yet not concerning the color of the skin, but of the color of the heart.

The line that separates America from itself runs through every individual race, society (culture) religion as well as politics, from top to bottom, from left to right. The chasm is growing wider and wider. Time is running out if this nation is to survive. We will exist as a geographical location only; "the land of the free, home of the brave" will become a fading memory.

I submit as proof of this growing rift is the fact that on the one hand some people are totally ignorant of what's really going on underneath the surface of America, or they simply don't care about anyone or anything but themselves, or they falsely accuse other people of what they are guilty of. The other group sees what's going on but have thus far not been able to figure out a strategy to close the rift, since the truth is hidden in plain sight, and lies are exposed in distorted blindness. In other words, lies rest on the surface and the truth dwells underneath. Like the tip of an iceberg, what is underneath is the real force to reckon with. The tip of the iceberg is that people tend to be highly superficial, self-absorbed, obsessed with "looks", money and power. They love to pretend, "act out", fantasize and otherwise overstate their importance (empty wagons make the most noise). Because of their love of lies, fiction, pretending, and playing make believe, they tend to be overly sensitive and emotional (feminine). Because of their lack of ability to balance between reality versus fantasy, truth versus lies, they tend to be either extremely passive or insanely violent. All of these qualities and characteristics will usually cause their lives to implode (unravel), stagnate or fragment. These Americans, though relatively few in number, yet because of their loud and incessant crying and whining, attract a lot of attention which they subtlety use to recruit more unsuspecting victims, by pity, violence, or downright lies.

The people beneath the surface tend to be quiet and invisible. They for the most part are the opposite of the "empty wagons." Since they love peace and harmony, they tend to be passive and subjective, not wanting to make waves or rock the boat. If America is going to survive it's time for the silent moral majority to awaken and arise to set the country back on its proper course. It is time for those that love reality, truth and America to rise up and let their voices be heard. Before it's not too late. Only time will tell.

The title of this little book *Let My People Go (Again!)* is actually a resonating, reverberating echo that not only speaks to my race, of whom I believe have been socially and politically engineered to stagnate, fragment, and finally implode. The title also resonates to my fellow Americans to not allow the force of "weakness" to pull this great nation apart, and drag it into darkness. The title also echoes as if the voice of God saying to His children to be free from the deceptive snare of the sin of this world (society). The reverberation shouts to every individual as well as the nation as a whole to strive to be as free, as whole and as one as possible.

Two nations for the price of one. A nation within a nation. One nation believes in and lives in a world of fiction (lies), emotionalism (femininity), slavery, fear, hate, and violence. The other nation believes in and lives in a world of reality (truth), intellectualism (masculine), freedom, courage, love, and peace.

I submit as the ultimate proof of these facts is this book itself. Some will read it and believe that it is truth. Others will read it and think that it is all lies. This will basically define which nation you belong to. Ultimately the truth will prevail because in the end there can be only one.

Having said that, if you would take a giant step back and look at America, you would see the country looks like and parallels a season of the television show 24. The cast of characters is huge, some 300 plus million. The roles that the characters play have a wide and varied range from super simple to highly complex. From major players to minor players, to cameo/walk-on roles, to stunt men and plenty of extras and back-grounders, to an ever expanding cast of black and white, and every color in between; men, women and children. The rich and the poor are represented, plus the young and the old. Legal immigrants and illegal aliens and Native Americans, which are expressed as politicians, business people, CEO's, a host of professionals from teachers, police, firefighters, soldiers, F.B.I., C.I.A., doctors, lawyers, judges, nurses, retail, sales, and customer service people and industry, construction to delivery and trucking industries to science and space programs to musicians and artists to restaurants and grocery store chains. To name only a few.

In this cast we see the portrayal of heroes, villains, thugs, and gangsters (political, religious and cultural), likewise the same for the pimps and hustlers. Housewives, mothers, daughters, sisters, aunts, nieces, harlots (Biblical definition) and fathers, husbands, sons, brothers, uncles, nephews, whoremongers (Biblical definition). Convicts, ex-convicts, saints, patriots, innocent bystanders, Capitalists, globalists, Socialists, communists, Marxists, Fascists, racists, bigots, insurgents, both foreign and domestic, as well as terrorists, sleeper cells, social and physical killers, traitors, turncoats, spies, "plants", haters, pacifists, apologists, instigators, clueless, global population controllers, environmentalists (whackos), heterophobes, feminists, sexists, etc.

The animal kingdom is well represented in this real life/fictional conspiracy. There are a number of snakes, jackals, wolves, moles, vultures, sitting ducks, lions, pussycats, foxes, dogs, doves, rats, eagles, sheep, lambs, hawks, sharks, pigs, stool pigeons, monkey-see-monkey-doers, monkeys that hear no evil, see no evil, and speak no evil. (Yeah, right!) As I said, there is a very large cast of characters with varied and complex roles to play, most playing multiple roles.

What role do you play? Do you love or hate America? How much? Do you have real love or superficial love for America?

In the interests of economics, this is my attempt at delivering you two books for the price of one. On the one hand, people see the glass as half empty, versus the people that see the glass as half full. The Bible puts it another way, "to the pure all things are pure, and the unclean all things are unclean." If you see the glass as half empty, then you probably don't really love America, do you? You probably want to make some type of major radical changes to this country instead of letting her continue to evolve on a true course of sound moral, social, economical, and political evolution. If you see the glass (America) as half full, then you probably do really love America and life as well realizing that as nations go, America is the best thing since sliced bread.

If this book were like the TV drama *24*, which is a parallel of a real American life crisis, then by the time you've finished reading this book, it would undoubtedly be time for the infamous Jack B interrogations to commence. It is go time! I have been doing this for a long, long time; it's like clock work to me. Once I find out what makes you "tick", I will know how to make you "tock." I predict that after 24 hours from reading this book, we will both know who you are and what role you have to play in all of this.

Right now we are at T minus zero hours and mark 00:00:00, 00:00:01, 00:00:02, 00:00:03, 00:00:04.

Question I:     Who are you really and what role do you have to play in this spiritual conspiracy?

Question II:     What do you know and when did you know it?

Question III:   Do you know or have you ever known what the definition of "is", is? YES OR NO?

Time check - 00:53:25

Question IV:   If you knew America was trapped between two spiritual black holes, one foreign and one domestic, what would you do?  WHAT WOULD YOU DO?

A)      Join the military?

B)      Join one of the black holes?

C)      Stick your head in the sand?

Time Check:   01:08:59

Question V:   Do you now or have you ever wanted to see America fall to the level of a third world nation as are cropping up on plantations all across the nation?

Time Check:   09:23:45

Question VI:   Do you want to see America keep moving forward or to see her fall backwards?

To be continued.

Time Check:   15:45:30

Question VII: If you are unhappy with this nation now, it will be many times worse if it is overrun by lawless law breakers.  THINK ABOUT IT!

Time Check:   21:34:55

Question VIII: Do you think that secular humanism is going to breed anything other than chaos and contention?  Too many little wannabe gods raising too many little banners, instead of raising one banner of the living God – LOVE OF TRUTH!

Time Check:   23:59:50

Question IX:   Okay, time is up, rummy.  Who are you and what's your role in all of this?  TELL US!  TELL US!!

# TABLE OF CONTENTS:

## INTRODUCTION

The times in which we live are "a changing," yet like in the words of a marriage vow, they are changing for "better or worse." This to me seems to be the crux of the problem, with so many issues, so many voices and opinions. The truth and the best direction for the nation can be so confusing, so complicated, that a large group of people are just tuning out.

This small book is a journal of what I see in my fellow Americans. The ones that see the change as a dream come true, and the others that see it as a nightmare unfolding, and last but not least, the totally clueless who can't figure out truth from lies; forward progress from backwards regression, those who can't see from left to right. This journal is written primarily for these people, to help them make up their hearts and minds.

Since the plot of our destiny is unfolding day by day, this is the first in a series to chronicle our ascent or decent into or from strength or weakness. These two words are the lowest and highest common denominators that define every man, woman, and child not only in America, but also in the world.

The book is definitive, but not exhaustive for time's sake, yet with enough desire you can extrapolate the direction of your life as well as that of the country and the world. Once you have read this book, either you will agree or disagree, which at the very least means you will no longer count as one of the "clueless" people in America. This is one view of one man of one nation of one word on one dream (American) of one life that we all must share. This book is a snapshot of the speed and power of the spiritual realm, so hold on tight.

# PREFACE

Let the Libs rue the day they thought to re-enslave my race and make them their foot-stool.

The Liberal Socialist Democrat Party has spiritually whipped and beaten my race so severely that after only 40 years in earnest the younger generations have gone and been driven functionally insane.

They glorify hate, lust, violence, murder, laziness, and deceit like it was something to be proud of. As if they are going to get away with doing "dirt". They are digging a spiritual, emotional, intellectual hole for themselves buried in muck and mire that one day they will wish they had not done. They even have "Toms and Tramps" in place to keep our youth hypnotized to destruction. The youth are the ones whom I battle for the most. They are mostly innocent.

"Younger generation, you need to look at the older ones. The reason you are in a bind is because your parents were following the 'Spiritually Dead.'"

The strong should always teach the weak. The downfall for Blacks in America was "dignity for dollars" i.e. entitlement programs welfare, etc. The Black race has been beaten so badly because of those Liberal Socialist programs it amazes me that Blacks still support the Democrats. Here is a short list of the severity of the spiritual, emotional, and psychological beatings we endure. Before I go there, let it be known, I am not some Oreo that likes to rag on his own race. My love is always towards my own.

We have been beaten so badly spiritually that most Blacks get mad at you when you even mention the truth or a different point of view, than that of a democratic perspective (subconsciously).

Most Blacks know nothing of the political process; they only know what they have been told to think: "Democrats good, Republicans bad." The vast majority doesn't even know what a filibuster is or (hit the mark with a hot one) a nuclear option (light up a block).

The point is that they don't know both sides of the coin.

The whole civil rights issue would have been rendered obsolete a long time ago if the people involved would have cared enough to follow the issues and vote accordingly (independence vs. dependence). We've been beat so bad they won't forgive people who have nothing to do with slavery, holding a grudge for centuries, but want to serve God?

Been beat so bad that a lot of Black men abandon their own kids to the world, and I have met some that won't even try to leave them some help (financially). I have heard them say, "Let them make it on their own the way I did" (mad at life and their parents).

Been beat so bad they want to party all the time (enough said).

Been beat so bad the president came out with a SSI plan to help us keep more money in our generations and Blacks still shot it down. Why? (Brain washed.) Let's not let the tragedy of slavery happen again. Okay!

Been beat so bad that when you are a part of Satan's kingdom, you actually cannot do damage to his kingdom no matter how much you jump, shout, "hoop and holler" and sing, or no matter how many pretty churches you build, nor based on the power of your vote. Jesus said that those that say, "Lord did we not do this, that and the other in your name?", and He said, "Depart from me; I never knew you." He is looking for those that worship Him in spirit and in truth.

The Libs live to strain the moral gnat and swallow the immoral camel (Matthew 23:24).

Since this chapter is spiritual, it's not like the "Libs" can actually take offense to it, unless they want to acknowledge God's Kingdom that they don't really believe exists.

This is a spiritual look from above.

The Libs' moral authority is in themselves which puts them on the same level as God. (FYI: That can't happen.) I hope after this you

Libs will have had enough of "playing God." You're not cut out for it. (Trust me.)

Everyone has a job to do in this world. My job is to grab the Liberal Socialist Democratic Party and shake it until everything that does not belong there falls off.

I think it would be a good idea to keep your house Negros, Uncle Toms and Aunt Jemimas on a short leash because there will probably be an angel of the Lord guarding the path of freedom for those that want to leave the plantations, and if they make too much noise they could be struck by a "sword" of the Lord.

All things return to their source: weakness to weakness, strength to strength, life to life, death to death.

The Libs "so called" moral equivalence is an affront to God. They starved Terri Schiavo to death, yet they would plea for a convicted killer's life. They kill unborn babies on a whim, yet they are nowhere near, nor anything like God at all.

Everybody is putting their two cents in, so I might as well throw my hat into the ring. America needs to have a dialogue to get to the bottom of what's wrong with the nation and what needs to be done to make it right. The longer we put it off, the weaker America will become. Let's not wait until it's too late.

---

**POP QUIZ:** In America, why do the rich get richer, and the poor get poorer?

**ANSWER:** Because, from a spiritual perspective, they are headed in two different directions...forward vs. backward, positive vs. negative, left vs.

---

## ROOTS

I have heard it said that desperate times call for desperate measures. I'm inclined to believe it is true, as witnessed by the start of the implosion of the Black race in America. With the advent of high-technology and a fast paced life-style, the rate of implosion is occurring exponentially. With 90% of Black Americans actively contributing to the rate of descent, this situation is spiraling out of control. Depending on what "spiritual plantation" you go to, as many as 70%, 80%, 90% of the Black youth are digging a spiritual hole for themselves, filled with hate, lust, violence, ignorance, anger, crime, drugs, laziness, fear, etc. Since they are our future, we are essentially helping them to self-exterminate our race.

If we leave and forsake them, where will we be as a people? I for one will not let this happen without the truth being known. If after reading these teachings you still wish to remain as you are, then don't complain about something you don't care enough to do anything about. I'm told the definition of insanity is doing the same thing over and over and expecting a different result.

# THE NITTY GRITTY

The following information that you are about to read is a spiritual look at Black America from above. The material will be enlightening to some, yet to others it will be upsetting, disturbing, or it may even anger, hurt, or offend.

The thing about these introductory chapters is that they were written last, and the main chapters were written first. This means that the introduction is the culmination of the chapters. To me this means there is no need for me to "beat around the bush." God wants me to give Him my all, which means to do the best I can to make the truth understood. So don't blame me; I'm just doing the job I was sent to do. Yeah that's right, this is the job I was sent to perform to the best of my ability. After having gone through a "living hell," and making it out alive and in my right mind, God gave me my purpose in life—the job He wants me to accomplish—now that I know who I am, where I come from, and where I am going. Yup, I just flew in from eternity and boy are my arms tired. (Joke)

Not that I'm perfect by any means, but since I do not fear death and am in defense of the truth, I have overcome the world. The reason I said death is because Satan will want to kill me for trying to tell you the truth. Since this is a volunteer army no one takes my life, I give it willingly for no greater love can a man have than to lay down his life, yet I know my Father has the power to give it back to me on the other side.

FYI: Only two kingdoms exist in the spiritual realm—the first one is of light, love, truth, strength and freedom (morality). The other is of darkness, hate, lies, weakness, and slavery (immorality). Since everything that pertains to mankind emanates from the spiritual realm, all of our thoughts our emotions and our creations both good and bad, have their source in the spiritual world and they return to their respective kingdoms, light or dark.

In the great nation of America we have a brilliant political system that provides for a way to administer checks and balances, yet all the while based on the principle that the majority has the right to rule based on the will of the people, by the awesome power of their vote. Prior to the 1960's, the two main political parties basically functioned as one. They sought to do what was best for the nation as a whole, and in the meantime evolving from some dark and hard times, i.e. slavery, World War I, II and The Great Depression.

But after the 60's the nation made a split. The "one political mind" became two distinct entities with two agendas that are completely opposite of each other. One is pulling to the "right" (clockwise) the other is pulling to the "left" (counterclockwise). One side is "Heaven straight" on the road to a positive future. The other side is "Hell bent" on the negative past. Of the two kingdoms, morality and immorality, which side believes in and supports killing unborn babies (to support the traditions of men)? They also support alternative lifestyles which contradict nature and God. They also support females that believe they are better suited to lead mankind regardless of God's ordained plan. They also believe that Government should take the place of God in the form of Socialism/communism. They also believe in starving Americans to death and letting convicted murderers live.

In case you did not know this is the Liberal Socialist regressive Democratic Party. The party of the immoral.

The Republicans are not perfect by any stretch. We all have faults and flaws to live and deal with, but just because we are not perfect does not mean that perfection (maturity) is not a goal worth striving for. When I look at the Republicans, I see people who like to make big money, have big clean fun, raise good smart kids, serve God, and try to help people in other parts of the world enjoy the freedom of life that God intended all men to enjoy. They believe in respect, valor, and honor (not all, but most). The thing I think is most important is that they believe in individual freedom and liberty which are derived from personal respect, responsibility, and discipline—which makes for small government, thank God.

# A NIGHTMARE ON AMERICAN STREETS

While I was working on this introduction, and trying to figure out the way to best describe the truth to you, I thought about Freddy Krueger's Nightmare on Elm Street series. Specifically how he was able to cause a person to dream when they fall asleep, and in some cases even when the person thought they were awake, they were actually still dreaming, still a part of his nightmare, his kingdom.

This is the exact same trick Satan uses to keep religious people in his nightmare. Just because you go to church and shout and sing and pray and then turn around and vote to keep his kingdom of immorality in power, you are still dreaming in his kingdom. He does not care what you say or do, or how many people you bring to church. You can't hurt or damage his kingdom at all, and in fact you cause it to grow.

Whose kingdom come? Whose will be done? If you want to do damage to his kingdom in America, then vote him out of office or just keep dreaming until your time runs out and it's time to wake up on the other side, and find the truth staring you dead in the face.

The Bible says, "Delight yourself in the Lord and He shall give you the desires of your heart" (Psalm 37:4). The desire of my heart is to see my race standing tall, free, brave, and saved.

## MORE ROOTS

Who in the world would have thought that we would be living in a new form of slavery in America, this is a spiritual form slavery, yet it is just as effective if not more so, than the old form due to the insidious, cover, and vast reach of spiritual slavery.

The reason most people can't see it is, as they say, "You can't see the forest for the trees." You either have to take some steps back or do like me and get a view from the top. Can you believe we have people who function in the roles and capacity of slave masters, house Negros, Aunt Jemimas, Uncle Toms, crops, plantations, and slave traders? If you take a few steps back and follow the power, the money, and the votes, you can see it for yourself.

The re-enslavement began in earnest back in the 1960s. Do you remember the mini-series "Roots," how they depicted the part when the slave master would teach a slave his or her name. He would tell the slave his "new" name. If the slave said his old name (i.e. Kunta-Kente), he was hit with a whip across the back again and again until the slave would finally give in and take his new name (Toby).

This is the same tactic the Liberal Democrats did to the Black race back in the 1960's. First they tied the Black woman to the post, and asked her ,"What do you need girl?" She answered, "My man, my kids and a home." Whap! Owner: "I said what do you need Kizzy?" Kizzy again states, "I said my man's arms around me, my babies and a home." Whap!! Owner: "All you need is this check, your kids, and a home. Now what do you need Kizzy?" Kizzy replies, "I told you—my man, my kids and a home." WHAP!!! Owner: "I told you all you need is this entitlement check, your kids and a home." This replays over and over and over, until she gives in and starts to accept the "new arrangement."

People can actually kill you with kindness.

After this was started, it was like a snowball rolling down the hill of time growing bigger and bigger until you get the disaster we have today. They did the same thing to the Black man as well. Owner: "What do you want to do with your life Toby?" Toby says, "I want a job, a wife, a home, and kids." Whap! Owner: "I said what do you want out of life Toby?" Toby replies, "A job, wife, kids, and home." Whap!! Owner: "No you don't Toby; you want to watch these Black exploitation films and learn how to oppress and abuse women—how to abandon your kids and home... Now what do you want Toby?" Toby: "I said a job, my woman, family, and home." Whap! Whap! Whap!! Owner: "Now Toby, I want you to take this weed and 40oz. (the Libs started the drug revolution of the 60's you know) and watch these Black exploitation movies and learn how to be a pimp, mack, gangster hustler, etc., and be an all around scourge to society." Over and over and over until Toby accepts the new way of doing things.

Just another snowball rolling down hill. And if that was not bad enough when our race tried to overcome and press on: WHAP! WHAP! WHAP!! WHAP! Owner: "You know, Toby and Kizzy, that you are disenfranchised victims and those people over there (Republicans) don't like you and are trying to hold you back. You had better stay on the plantation where we can protect you and take care of you." The same lies told over and over again until it is believed by up to 90% of Black Americans to this day. So many lives, families, homes, dreams, and potential wasted, destroyed. The Bible says even "Satan appears as an angel of light" and if it were possible could fool the very elect (2 Corinthians 11:14).

## THE HEEL VS. THE HEAD

If you were in a life or death fight with an adversary, would you want to bruise his heal or his head? To bruise his heel would be like having a busted pipe at home and instead of fixing the problem you just keep cleaning up a mess all day everyday. If you bruise the "head" then the problem will be solved. If we could overcome our pride and our self-pity, we would find ourselves in the center of God's will. We would then be in a position to help each other overcome all obstacles; "united we stand, divided we fall."

To all the religious people on the Left, I think you should turn on the light and see who you are in bed with spiritually, politically and culturally. Talk about "sleeping with the enemy." Where would we be if Jesus felt sorry for and took pity on Satan? The best way to help people who are down on life is not to climb into the "mud" with them. You should leave the light on so they can find the steps to climb out of the pit for themselves, because like 'Harry Hippy', you can't help someone who wants to sleep on the ground.

God knows that tough love can make you feel bad, guilty, and ashamed for being hard on people who are already down and out, but two wrongs don't make a right, and misery loves company. Someone has to be Toby, the adult. (Maturity)

# THE SPIRITUAL WARFOOTING OF AMERICA

That which you are about to read is a real life, real time battle assessment of and for America. As I write this, it is 8-22-06. The United States of America is now prosecuting two wars at the same time. One battle is ideological, spiritual, and domestic. The other is physical, spiritual and foreign. Both enemies of the country emanate from the same source. The best bet to win these wars is to stop the enemy within first. The only difference between the two enemies is literally a matter of time.

In the entire universe, both physical and spiritual, there are two forces that shape and govern everything including man. Those two forces are strength vs. weakness. These powers that make the world go round and expressed in different forms such as: Truth vs. Lies; Love vs. Hate; Life vs. Death; Light vs. dark; Hot vs. Cold; Good vs. Evil; Hard vs. Soft; Moral vs. Immoral; Faith vs. Fear; Masculine vs. Feminine; Intellect vs. Emotion; Spiritual vs. Physical; Forward vs. Backward, and last but not least Right vs. Left.

# THE GATEWAY TO THE ABYSS

They say that there is a thin line between sanity and insanity; the door to the abyss, the gateway to insanity is self–pity. Everything in life including life itself is positive (it beats being dead). But, when a person or race or religion or country starts to feel sorry for itself, the flow of life is reversed from positive to negative, from forward to backward, from outward to inward, from intellect to emotion, from masculine to feminine, from strong to weak.

When a person, race, or religion suffers a defeat or rejection in life, they cross the line instead of seeing life as a gift and a blessing; the way God intended. Instead, they open up a vortex of implosion inside their souls. Since we are all self-contained beings, our life is expressed in a time line from cradle to grave. The easiest way to visualize this dynamic is to look at a clock on a wall. When the hands move to the "right," they move in a positive direction, forward, into the future, growing stronger and stronger. Yet when those hands move to the Left, a person moves in reverse. Picture a cone moving in a spiral to the Left. The numbers are now negative, the direction is backwards, and the time line is moving towards the past; instead of moving towards life, it moves towards death.

Once a person or group views themselves as victims, they can justify any crime, any act of depravity, because to them it's not their fault. After all, they are the victims. They express all manner of unforgiveness, hate, jealousy, anger, violence, lust, greed, revenge, laziness and deceit. These people become so selfish that they think the world revolves around them.

If you look at every faction on the Left, in this country and around the world, they all have that one thing in common. They all "feel" sorry (weak) for themselves, and their number one person to blame is someone on the right. They can't stand to see people happy and successful when they are not. As previously mentioned, misery loves company. The reason that the Left cannot see the extreme danger the nation is in from terrorism, is because in the spiral effect of the cone. The radicals have been moving backwards for centuries, so they are actually behind the Libs in this country. However, both are focused on the object of their hate for America. The Libs will not turn around and see what's behind them. It's like why Dracula cannot see himself in the mirror; evil cannot see itself for what it is (after all, evil is the victim).

A civilized society vs. an uncivilized one: the choice is yours and mine. I am a Black Christian, conservative, patriot. I am a highly trained spiritual observer/strategist. My heavenly father has sent me into the battle to see if the nation will turn from left to right, from backwards to forwards as a whole nation. "Judgment Day" is moving closer and closer.

Based on the weak, ignorant state of the nation, tragedy is almost inevitable. How long and how severe remains to be seen. It is for this reason I am extremely concerned about my race, who have been turned back into slavery complete with slave masters, house Negroes, Aunt Jemimas, Uncle Toms (gangster rappers), slave traders, crops, plantations, slave drivers and overseers. The entire religious left is under the authority of the Queen of Heaven, (Jeremiah 44). She is second in command under Satan. They think that they are moving forward, yet because of unforgiveness and bitterness of the past, they are moving backwards with the rest of the Left. They are basically doing the M.J. moonwalk (he-he!!).

## DEATH BY 1,000 KNIVES VIA POLITICAL CORRECTNESS

The left, both nationally and internationally and with the help of the media, has used political correctness as a mobile siege on the Right's spiritual fortress bit by bit, and little by little. They are closing in. They have the Right surrounded as racist, sexist, bigots, and homophobes. Their goal is to remove God, the true and living God, from the nation and world. The battle for civilization has begun in earnest.

T.M.A.: "too much analysis" from the White House to the Republican base to talk radio. The Republicans are true to form— "reactionary" analyze this, analyze that; as if analyzing everything was going to solve anything. You know the truth. Question is, what can we do to help? The clock is ticking either backwards or forwards.

This is an assessment of the nation. It is an outline to a book as well. The civilized rights movement has come full circle.

# FOOD FOR THOUGHT

*The Last God Standing*

I imagine the way to see who will win this war is to see which side will be forced to lose faith in their god first.

*Speed vs. time*

Since weakness, sin and evil are so mesmerizing, so progressive and so debilitating, we have speed on our side and time is on their side.

*Feel vs. think*

Everyone is born knowing how to feel (to think selfishly), yet people must learn or be taught how to "think" or to put others first (selfless).

*See Dick and Jane run, run, run*

Since Jesus was and is a perfect man, in His masculinity as well as being God (love, truth, and life), He is pure power and pure light. If a man runs towards Jesus, he will be made more like Him; light, power, love, truth and life. If you run from Him as a man, you become more feminine, weak, deceived, in darkness, and you will bend over for anything. Likewise, if a woman runs toward Jesus, she will become more feminine, soft, loving, kind, wise, etc. If a woman runs away from Jesus, she becomes more masculine, rough, bitter, angry, apathetic, cynical, and skeptical, etc. That's why "Hell hath no fury like a woman scorned," if her tender heart is broken. So Dick and Jane, which way are you running?

*Oh where oh where has my little god gone? Oh where oh where can he be?*

God is not little and He has not gone anywhere. God is in the "action," the split second you decide to take action by faith. For the truth, He's there. So by faith He will be as big or small as you make Him.

*Steel sharpens steel*

You cannot sharpen a knife with marshmallows. The reason the Republicans are spending like "drunken sailors," and the reason they won't fix the war on terror effectively, is because there is no checks and balances. The Libs want to bring America down any way. Talk about "two birds killing one stone."

*The enemy of my enemy is my friend.*

Yet, in spiritual warfare, knowing who your enemy is vs. who is your friend can be difficult.

*A note on weakness*

To tolerate weakness, sin, or evil in you, or in society, is to welcome yours and our demise. Being intolerant of weakness is a good thing.

*Civil rights vs. Civilized right*

The former group needs someone to stand up for them. The latter group knows and cares enough about themselves to stand up for themselves.

*Son light*

The best bet for America is the "son light" of the truth to disinfect the darkness of lies.

*To vote or not to vote*

For the conservative Republicans who are thinking about not voting, to teach the Republicans a lesson, to them I say, "Learn the lesson of the rope in gym class." This is the rope you had to climb to the top. Not voting or voting left would be like climbing 5 feet from the top and then stopping to rub your hands together to get a better grip, (don't be stupid).

*Un-funny*

The biggest joke of the century that is not funny, an unjoke, is the U.N. They make a habit of bombing out like with U.N Resolution 1701.

## Embrace the force

You cannot kick against the goads of life, for that would be God, and it's useless and dangerous. The force of life is positive and moves forward.

## Some Definitions

According to Webster's New World Dictionary and Thesaurus copyright 2002, the definition of "Left" is: adjective, i.e. left, weak one, of or on the side that is toward the west when one faces north (upward, God). Too often in politics, a Liberal or "radical" position, party, etc.

"Radical" synonyms: militant, recalcitrant, mutinous, seditious, riotous, lawless, racist, insubordinate, anarchistic, unruly, nihilistic, communistic, socialist, traitor, mutineer, extremist, fascist, nazi, iconoclast, hippy, fanatic, etc.

"Right": straight, upright, virtuous, correct, fitting, suitable, designating the side or surface meant to be seen, mentally or physically sound, designating or have the side of the body toward the east when one faces north (God), (related to politics: a conservative or reactionary position party according to law, justice, righteousness, etc.)

The sun rises in the east (light, strength and right). The sun sets in the west (darkness, weakness and left). If it were up to the Libs, they would reverse the very order of the universe. They would rather darkness and weakness come first before light and strength.

Everything that you think, say and do emanated from the spiritual realm of your mind. Including what you do with what you just read. Relax; God can only hold you accountable for what you know.

## JUST IN CASE YOU ARE STILL HUNGRY, HERE'S SOME MORE FOOD FOR THOUGHT

- It is ironic and hypocritical to help Iraq and Afghanistan. We help them rid themselves of the weakness in their midst, and yet cower from the weakness in our own country.

- Learn the lesson of the Lebanese. See what happens to people who are too afraid to deal with weakness in themselves and consequently in their midst.

- One good insurgency deserves another. The United States has a reputation for planning insurgencies of weak evil regimes and rightly so, such as the one being contemplated in Iran. We need an insurgency in America to unseat, uproot and defeat Leftism (weakness) in this country before it's too late.

- Libs are Americans by birth, not by spirit (of America).

- Denial is a river that runs through the heart of Egypt. Question is, does it run through your heart as well?

- The final solution, funds. Suggested names: "America's 1st Fund," "Americans United Fund," "Celebrate America Fund," "The Choice of America Fund," or "American Spirit Fund." All conservative talk radio hosts set up a fund and take donations from their audiences. On the surface, help college students and K-12. Meanwhile, organize and mobilize behind the scenes, helping to fund people or groups to drive the Leftist out of the Democratic Party.

- The definition of schizophrenia is the separation of thought and emotion. This is the problem America suffers from left (emotion) vs. right (thought). The problem with this problem is that our enemy abroad is not so schizo.

- The saddest and weakest sight I have ever seen is a Black American communist.

- My definition of a moderate is a headless body looking for one—a head that is.

- Can anyone please explain to me how that at present the past is on a collision course with the future?

- Never mind if it walks like a duck and quacks like a duck…all I want to know is can a duck walk in two directions at that same time? (forward vs. backward). And can it quack (talk) both strength and weakness at the same time?

## MORE FOOD FOR THOUGHT, THE MAIN COURSE (FILET MIGNON)

1.  The intelligence of weakness has specific attributes like being subversive, deceptive, destructive, and deadly.

2.  The intelligence of strength has specific attributes as well, like being solidifying, upright, honest, constructive and lively, (life giving).

3.  The self-hate of the Left will get us all killed.

4.  The self-righteousness of the Right will get us all killed.

5.  Trying to guess whether God is telling the truth or not i.e. "The Bible" is like playing Russian roulette with a two-barrel revolver. 50/50 odds are not that great. When you consider, you might spend an eternity losing all your marbles.

6.  The truth is the light of the soul. Since crap rolls down hill, it's not a bright or intelligent idea for people at the bottom of the social economic/cultural ladder to vote to pull the nation down on their own heads.

7.  If a person (you) wanted to cut to the chase and break the Bible, yourself, and all of life and everyone in it, to its lowest and highest common denominators, you would find strength vs. weakness. As a matter of fact, the Bible is a snapshot of the history of this fact. Since the two forces have intelligence involved, the following examples must be seen as in a struggle, (vice versa). Example, Truth vs. Lies—Lies vs. Truth, so consequently in effect, a person is playing Russian roulette with a two-barrel revolver. Through the power of your free will, you can choose Heaven vs. Hell, God vs. Satan, Life vs. Death, Lawful vs. Lawless, Spiritual vs. Physical, Light vs. Dark, Forward vs. Backward, Intelligence vs. Ignorance, Hate vs. Love, Hot vs. Cold, Man vs. Nature, Faith vs. Doubt, Courage vs. Fear, Intellect vs. Emotion, Good vs. Evil, Powerful vs. Powerless, Masculine vs. Feminine, Right vs. Wrong, A

man vs. Himself, Selfless vs. Selfish, Responsible vs. Irresponsible, Discipline vs. Undisciplined, Respectful vs. Disrespectful, A man vs. A man, A man vs. A woman, A religion vs. A religion, A race vs. A race, A village vs. A village, A nation vs. A nation, Rich vs. Poor, Civilized vs. Uncivilized, Sanity vs. Insanity, and finally (last but not least), the struggle that actually sums up all the rest, the clock on the wall tells it all. The directions that express the total potential (positive or negative) and destiny of man is left vs. right. The hands of a clock move forward (increase upward) positively to the right. If the hands were to move backwards (decrease downward), they would move negatively to the Left. Like it nor not, it's just that simple. It's time to get back to the basics.

# THE HOCUS POCUS PARTY

Ladies and gentlemen, children of all ages, it is my dubious honor to present to you the greatest company of magicians and illusionists America and the world has ever seen: The one, the only, the infamous Liberal Democratic party (Boo's).

This news may come as a shock to you as it did me, being a Black man who like the vast majority of my race (90%) has given the Lib Dems a big Black blank check to control and dictate our every thought, word and deed as it pertains to strength and weakness. (A slave cannot be stronger than his master.)

It is like they say, "if you can't see the forest for the trees" it's because you are too close. In order to see clearly, you need to take a few hundred steps back so you can get a clear view of both parties. This is what I saw when I looked left. The Lib Dems makes lousy politicians, yet they are the undisputed masters of ledger-domain. They will promise you the world, but all you will end up with is a hand full of dirt.

{Queue the magician theme music}

<Dim the lights>

Now without further ado, I give you the spin gollies of our age. The Houdini's of this lifetime: "the Lib Demoniacs."

1. Now for their first trick that began in earnest in the 60's, the Libs are attempting to saw America in two. Instead of parties doing what's best to move the nation forward, the Libs have spiritually turned left and are actively seeking to take the nation backwards in time. They accomplish this by capitalizing and profiting on the inevitable chaos, confusion, misery, and hopelessness that occurs anytime there is a split in a nation, race, or a person. Thus far, the Libs have divided the races, the sexes, the classes (rich vs. poor), the generations, (young vs. old). (United we stand, divided we fall.) The clock on your wall tells the truth. The hands move to the right: forward, positive, future,

strong. If they did move left: backwards, negative, past weak; you decide.

2.  Now for their next trick: the art of "slight of hand." While the Libs have distracted their base by pointing the finger of blame on the right hand, no one is paying attention to what they are doing on the "left." Their base has become "a useful idiot," helping the Libs accomplish their goals. They are so consumed with their own petty and selfish demands, that they cannot see how the Libs are desperately seeking to undermine the foundational framework that keeps America strong and free.

    A.) Their base cannot see how the Libs attack the judicial system via activist judges who seek to interpret the law and the constitution based on their mixed-up feelings, which change with the wind instead of the truth which never changes.

    B.) They are also blind to see how Libs are destabilizing society and the family unit through immoral behavior— transmitted from MTV, rap music videos, TV programming, movies, magazines, etc.

    C.) They cannot understand how the Libs (via the ACLU) are trying to isolate and marginalize the real God and church. They don't pay mind to fake ones because they are harmless and weak. If the Lib base thinks they have something to cry about now, compared to the poor people in the rest of the world, God is going to really give them something to cry about.

3.  Now for their next trick. Levitation—the Libs via materialism: cars, rims, sound systems, clothes, jewelry, cash, motorcycles, drugs, and sex combined with the media, music, rap, rock, videos, and games (the usual suspects). The Libs have succeeded in filling the younger generations' head with so much nonsense (weakness), that they have lost touch with reality (truth). They are floating on a cloud nine, actually acting like they will get away with

being dirty and lazy.  They are being cool, sexy, tough, and acting like the aforementioned are the most important things in life (float on).

*30-minute intermission*

Now back to the show:

4.  The Libs are never at a loss.  They always have a trick or two up their sleeves.  How about the trick they played on Black people?  The Libs said that they would pull us out of poverty, like a magician pulling a rabbit out of his hat.  Yet, in spiritual reality, they've pulled us out of the frying pan and dumped us into the fire of spiritual weakness, which is condemning my race to live out the role of a slave on a plantation.  Abracadabra!

5.  Now for their Grande Finale!  Based on how they have weakened and demoralized the nation, and brainwashed our kids K-12 as well as most college students, in combination with their weak, pacifistic stance on world terrorists, the Libs are seeking to make America disappear.  We may still be here geographically, as in every man, woman and child will have the body of a human, but the head of a jackass for allowing these illusionists to take this great nation from us and wreck it. WELL THAT'S ALL FOLKS!

P.S.  I believe that there is still time to pull the curtain down on these spin gollies before they bring the house (America) down on all of our heads.

He-haw…He-haw!!!

P.P.S.  Make up your mind, then make a move.  The clock is ticking either backwards or forwards.  Which way are you headed?

The Black Patriot

Okay, one more P.S.:  If you can believe, if you care, then circulate this show.  If not, then suppress it.  It will be between you and God.

# THE NEMESIS CODE

*The line, the clock and the cross*

Spiritual ceilings are harder to break than glass or corporate ones

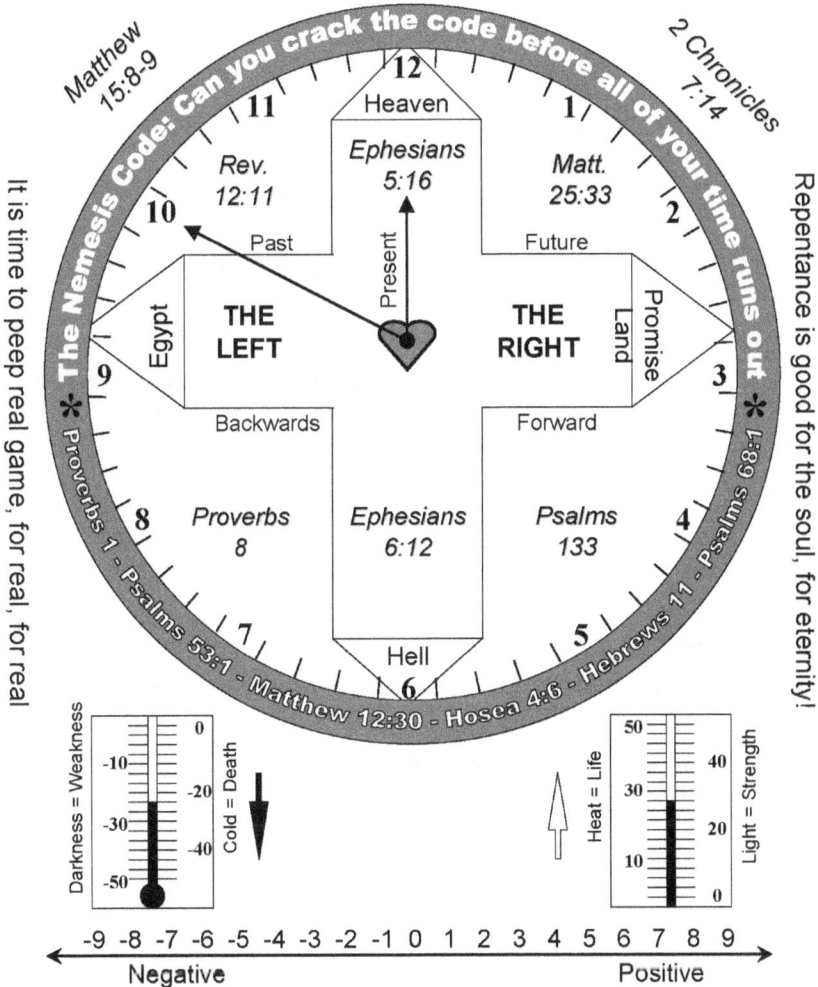

If the spiritually blind lead the blind, they will both fall into a ditch

Either this is just a piece of paper you are holding with some symbols and words and Bible verses on it, or this is the single most powerful instrument you may ever possess, able to turn your life around, or a race or a nation.  This is the difference between the spiritual and physical realm.  The power of the truth is awesome.  The powers of lies are awesome as well.  The key to life is to be able to distinguish between the two.  This is the reason the Nemesis Code was created, for "you."  The Nemesis Code (N.C.) is spiritual, and the arrows on the line and the cross go on from here to eternity.  The hands on the clock are moving either forward or backward depending on the direction of your life.

The "code" was designed to help you determine whether you are friend or foe to yourself, God and your fellow man.  The "spiritual right" seem to equal that friend and foe respectively.

If it is true that birds of a feather flock together, then it stands to reason that everything calls to its own.  Deep calls to deep, and shallow to shallow.  It also stands to reason that every thing returns to its own; ashes to ashes, dust to dust, life to life and death to death.  The stakes of your decisions are high and costly, so choose well.

The little heart in the center is the place where all the issues of your life will spring from, whether they are of the truth or lies.

Since no man or woman is an island unto himself or herself, what you do with the truth and lies can make a difference not only in your life, but also in the lives of your family, friends, co-workers, and strangers.  If you have children, you will influence them more than anyone else.  Their potential future is in your hands.  So if you care, pay close attention.  Your child's future could be at stake.

If you are like most people I know, you got a big kick out of the old TV series "The Twilight Zone."  Yet, I know another zone where the vast majority of Americans like to dwell; it's called "The Mediocrity Zone."  Never mind where's the beef, where's the passion for life?  People in the "M.Z." seem to be perfectly content just going through the motions of living in such a way as to blend in with everyone else around them.  It is like a dance.  They take two steps up and two steps back.  If you look at the number line, that would keep you right about at zero.  That's why so many Americans get bored with life so easily.  You have so much to do, but if you don't have a goal or direction in life, nothing really matters.

Life is positive and it's a gift. As seen through positive eyes, the opposite of life is death, so we can assess that life was meant to be lived positively. Where the numbers move higher and higher is to the "right."

If you look at the line from a vertical viewpoint, it would take the form of a thermometer. As the numbers go up, they indicate strength, heat, light and life—as opposed to going in the other direction, where the numbers indicate weakness, darkness, cold and death.

Looking at the "cross" from a biblical perspective, the children of Israel had to move forward to get to the "Promised Land." If they had gone backwards, it would have lead to slavery and bondage in Egypt. Is that where you want to be?

Can you drive a car? Well what about your life? I have never seen a person drive a car in reverse (backwards) to get to where they are going ahead (forward). Time moves forward not backwards. You are getting older not younger, so get your life in the "right" gear and get moving...and for God's sake, watch where you are going. Oh, by the way, this is why people in reverse usually go out of the world a—backwards. BEEP! BEEP!

If a person chooses to keep going in reverse they will become more immature vs. mature. Today, being spoiled (immature) is in style, yet like most things that are useless, they get dumped sooner or later. So if you are done looking in the rearview mirror of life, we can move on.

To be or not to be, that is the question. To explode with positivism or to implode with negativity is the choice. Is it time to choose yet? It's your life isn't it? Well, time will tell.

Your life is filled with potential. You can do just about anything that you have the faith to believe you can (as a man thinketh in his heart so is he). Your life is a spiritual hurricane like the hands on the clock moving forward (positive) around and around, seconds,

61

minutes, hours, days, weeks, months, years and decades. The more you stay positive in your thoughts, words, feelings and actions, the stronger you will grow physically, spiritually, emotionally and intellectually as you let go of all your negativity, fear, doubt, hate, lust, laziness, jealousy, unforgiveness, pride, selfishness, etc.

The more positive you become the more positive effect you will have on the people around you: family, friends, co-workers, and strangers. It will eventually have an effect (positive) on their lives, their friends and family, and so on and so on. Likewise, if you implode, you will drag other people into your nightmare around and around, deeper and deeper, darker and darker, weaker and weaker. This implosion can happen to an individual, a race, a nation or a religion (hint, hint).

I hate to split hairs, yet that's what I am authorized to do. This is the thin line between love and hate, sanity and insanity.

Since the universe and nature abhors (hates) a vacuum, and since there are not that many whole-hearted (positive) people in the world, negativity and weakness fill the void. This is why you really, really need to get down on your knees and thank God for Jesus. He is the only real counter point to all of the negativity in the world. That's why we need to follow Him only. He's the only one that can save us from our sins, this world and the Devil. The Lord is knocking on the door of your heart. Are you going to get that?

The purpose of life is to be at peace with God, yourself and your fellowman. Anything you do that's negative means you have work to do. No one is perfect, yet there is plenty of room for improvement.

Like an airplane trying to take off with too much weight on board, you have to lighten your load (negativity), and then you can fly. Okay, it's time for a test flight. Are you ready? Don't be nervous. You'll do fine…I hope…Just kidding!

Pre-trip flight inspection. Anxiety comes from getting ahead of yourself, and then comes frustration, anger, depression and failure.

So step one: <u>be still</u> and know that God is in control. Ask Him to show you all or some of the weaknesses that you need to deal with. Look at what you think about, how you feel and how you feel about what you think. This will help you to find and to focus your passions. Step two: <u>crawl</u>. Move slowly and stay low. Start moving, read your Bible, and pray as much as possible. Step three: <u>walk</u> when you get stronger and can keep your balance. Step four: <u>run</u> slow, then faster and faster. The final step: spread your wings and <u>fly</u> as long and as far as you can, and if you fall, get up as fast as possible and try again and again. Never, never, never give up on yourself. Well, those are the basics of Human Flight, (spiritual anyway). Do you believe you can fly? Can you touch the sky?

One other thing, the Nemesis clock is pointing to ten to midnight. It's getting dark out here. We could use some more light. Like a campfire there are three components to make the fire burn, wood (combustible), oxygen (precipitant), and the spark (igniter). God is trying to set your soul on fire for the truth, people (combustible), life (precipitant), and your faith (igniter).

Okay, pop quiz. Whatcha' holdin' is a single piece of paper in your hands, or is it something a whole lot more? The fruit of the spirit is love, joy, peace, long suffering, gentleness, faith, meekness, and temperance. The power of the truth is awesome. What if you gave this code to 50, 100 or 1,000 people and they did the same, and so on. The right path of the code can be known, but it cannot be cracked because every moment, day, week, month and year can change. That's how God made it to keep you interested and on your toes.

ENJOY LIFE – <u>BE BORN AGAIN</u>!

# NATURE, PSYCHOLOGY AND DILEMMA OF SIN

*The Nature of Sin*

What is sin? Where did it come from? Who is guilty of it? Why does it have such a negative reputation? Why do some people believe and don't believe in its existence? Does your belief make any difference in your life and subsequently the world (life) that we all share?

These are just a few of the questions that we will look at, and attempt to answer. I believe the obvious place to start is with the Bible (the Word of God). For that is where we are introduced to the whole concept of sin. According to the Bible, God created man in His own image with the ability to think, feel, will and create. In the Garden of Eden, man had total reign. He had peace and harmony with God, Himself and His environment. He was even at one with the woman that God had made for him. There was only one rule that God gave man, and that was not to eat from the tree of knowledge of good and evil.

To make a long story short, the woman was deceived into eating that forbidden fruit which she also gave to her husband and he ate of the knowledge of good and evil. This is where sin entered into man's world—through disobedience to the will of God. Since God is the source of life itself, to disobey (reject) His will is to separate oneself from the life in the spiritual. The other component to man being created in God's image is that we are spirits wrapped (housed) in bodies of flesh and blood.

Since the opposite of life is death, man began a perpetual state of falling away (dying) spiritually and because everything man does emanates from the spiritual realm, the dying effect is manifested in every aspect of a man's being; his thoughts, his feelings, his words, as well as his actions. Since the opposite of life is death, we must conclude that life is positive and death is negative. In man's rebellion, he has created a void (rift) in his relationship to life (God) which in his heart is expressed as a hole or feeling of emptiness. Man longs to be filled with what's missing, namely

God, yet since man has the knowledge of self (good and evil) in accordance with his fallen away, negative condition, man seeks to fill his emptiness with all manner of selfish endeavors from politics, relationships, careers, material things, power, money, sex, fame, religion, sports fitness, etc…which in and of themselves may not be bad or wrong except when you make them your god to worship or be worshipped by others.

This condition puts man in direct confrontation with God, since life is positive, expanding up, outward and forward, e.g. a blade of grass, a tree, the birth of a baby, or the universe. All positive things in life increase and bear fruit. Yet on the other hand things with no life in them are in a state of dying. In man this is revealed in negative destructive and violent behavior.

Therefore I conclude, the nature of sin is to subtract, divide and retract (implode). Implosion is the best way to describe man's perpetual state of falling away from God.

*The Psychology of Sin*

The unregenerate man is in a constant state of dying spiritually, hiding from and rejecting the will of God. Based on mankind's selfish, apathetic inharmonious behavior, I think the best way to sum up his condition is to say he is suffering in a state of chronic spiritual inferiority. Since man severed ties with God he has been in a constant state of trying to measure up to His (God's) standards or to replace God altogether (idolatry). In either case the attempt is a study in futility.

The term "inferiority" means low quality, below standard, poor, weak, or inadequate. The word complex in this case seems to indicate a group of components or characteristics that support and animate the inferiority in a man's heart. After much thought and consideration, the three elements of man's condition in my humble opinion are fear, lies, and ignorance. These three components form a cycle that is expressed in man as a downward spiral of negativity, weakness, and defeat. This condition is most clearly seen in a person's life that is spinning out of control.

Yet some people are able to keep a facade of being in control on the outside, while feeling the same effect on the inside. The result will be the same separation from God forever, whether fast or slow. The wrong road will never lead to the right direction; since God is positive, He's moving forward in the right direction. If man is moving in the opposite direction that means he's degenerating, going backwards in the wrong direction (left), becoming weaker, being more unstable, and detaching from reality.

Since the split, man is being bombarded with choices between good and evil, to move forward in life (positive) or backward (negative). Also, the two facets that express the sum total of a man's life are intellect (think) or emotion (feel). The strong side of man is his ability to think, the weak side is to feel.

The strong side of man's intellect is positive and moves him in a forward direction. The weak side (left) does the opposite. This side tends to move inward, backwards and is selfish; in other words negative. If the latter condition controls a man or woman, it begins a cyclone fueled by fear, lies, and ignorance, then giving way to fear of God, himself, and fellowman, eventually breeding distrust, anger, and frustration, which is multiplied by lies on our origin, potential, and purpose, creating even more chaos combined with ignorance. The situation grows exponentially to become a humongous swirling spiritual black hole of wickedness pulling at every new life that comes into the world. Since the fall of Adam, all men after him have the inherent propensity to sin, implode, and become selfish and apathetic. This is the condition known as "Fallen Man." He is perpetually falling away from God.

The good news is the opposite of this cycle of death, is the cycle of life which is truth, faith, and knowledge. The best way to understand both cycles is to view them as spiritual fires, one of death and one of life. Like the fires we see in our everyday life they each have three components that work in unison. To start and maintain itself, spiritual fire as well as natural fire are identical in that one can be used for good (heating our homes, cooking our food, driving our cars, planes, boats, and trains), or it can be used to destroy (burning down homes, people, forests, etc.) The key to determining between the two is to know whether the fire is under control or not. In either case, spiritual or natural, intellect (thought) keeps a fire under control.

On the other hand, a destructive fire is out of control emotions (feelings). The two fires of man are thought and feeling. The right side of man as he is facing north is his strong side; intellect is on the east side, where the sun rises. The weak side of man as he faces north is the Left. The sun sets in the west.

This is the epic struggle we face in ourselves, our country and the world; the battle between strength and weakness, good and evil, forward and background, God and Satan.

*The Dilemma*

Now that man has opened Pandora's box and acquired the knowledge of good and evil (truth and lies), he finds himself locked in an eternal struggle with himself, God and Satan. He must decide whether to believe what God says in His word, or to go it alone, which is to agree with Satan.

"To be or not to be." To humble yourself or to remain proud, that is the question. A man's pride is the #1 obstacle that keeps him from being reunited with God. Pride is what got Lucifer tossed out of Heaven and it is what will get man tossed into Hell. This is the dilemma. This is why God had to send his only begotten son Jesus the Christ to save mankind from himself. Yet, because of pride some people still refuse to believe unto their own destruction. What will you decide? What kingdom will you serve: light or darkness? The nature of sin is to subtract, divide, and retract (implode). The nature of righteousness is to add, multiply, and expand. Which do you think would make for a happier life, and a better world for us to live in? With your vote, you can make the choice.

## THE KEY

After you have given the matter of your life some serious thought and are willing to swallow your pride, and if you DARE to turn the key to turn your life around to activate "the code" to see just how very much God loves you, you may find that your purpose in life is to fulfill and reach your destiny so that your true potential may be manifested to the world.

If you wish to know what it means to be "born again," to have a second chance at life, then you need to make a list of all your weak, negative and sinful thoughts, feelings, words, attitudes, actions and habits. From pride to low self worth, from hate to greed, from lust to selfishness, from apathy to envy, from ingratitude to indifference, plus your fears, doubts and worries. Then ask God, in the name of Jesus, by the power of the Holy Spirit, to come into your heart and life. Ask him to separate you, forgive you, cleanse you and save you, heal and restore you from all of your darkness; only then you will know that the meaning of life is to know life (GOD). Some of your issues will be harder to face then others. Some days will be better than others. Yet, "He" will always be with you, and you are guaranteed the victory over all, which is the salvation of your soul.

P.S. Join a real church. Pray and read your Bible, and live it as much as possible.

God Bless

# HOW TO REVIVE A NATION (USA)

To the churches that are in or near the inner cities all across America, greetings to you and peace in the name of the Lord and Savior Jesus Christ.

The information contained in this letter is the culmination of my twenty-year quest, which I have embarked upon in search of the truth, the meaning of life, and the Will of God. This is my assessment of my adventure. The journey began halfway around the world while stationed in Hawaii. I was twenty years of age, and in the U.S. Navy. I was given the opportunity to work and meet people from all over the world—from Hong Kong to Madagascar, people from all walks of life, colors, creeds, races and religions.

While embarked on my God-inspired journey, I ran the gamut of human experience. At various times in my life I have been rich and poor (relatively speaking), weak, strong, leaned to the Left and right, pulled, stretched, smashed, twisted, been hot and cold, gone in circles, seen highs and lows, dwelt in light and deep darkness, gone back and forth, from side to side, intellectual and emotional I've been right and wrong, believed truth and lies. After twenty years of searching for purpose and meaning in life, here is what God taught me.

1. He's real

2. He loves us

3. He loves us very much

4. In order to experience His love you must obey Him

5. In accordance with these truths you can only travel in two directions in life, they are either forwards or backwards.

Whether you know it or not, whether you care or not, whether you are deceived or not, here lies wisdom. Time stands still for no man, even if you don't feel your life moving at all. Time is moving you, shaping you to grow either inward (backward), or outward (forward). Trying to remain neutral or living in the middle of the road (lukewarm-ness) is impossible. Walking a tightrope or standing on the fence is useless and time consuming. Either you are moving towards the true and living God or you are moving away from him. One road is broad and wide leading away, and the other is straight and narrow leading towards Him (God).

Now having said all of that, let's get down to brass tacks where the rubber meets the road. That's where your life and my life intersected, since no man is an island. We all have an effect on each other, either directly or indirectly, to move civilization either forward or backwards.

The United States is presently divided into two parties, Democrats vs. Republicans, Liberals vs. Conservatives, the Right vs. the Left. In the natural course of evolution both parties are headed in two different directions each with its own set of values, ideologies, rules and ethics. This rift is causing our nation to split, thereby becoming more unstable and dangerous. According to the Bible, a house or a nation divided against itself cannot stand (Mark 3:25), therefore it is of the utmost importance for Americans to figure out which direction is best for the nation instead of self, that the country can be reunited so that she may continue to grow.

After all of the training God put me through, here is the solution He gave me, to avoid this pending crisis. There are now some 300 hundred million people in the United States, 23% of which is African-American, 90% of which is said to vote leftist. Since we make up a very large portion of the Nation, as we go, so goes the Nation, weak or strong, forward or backwards. Your life is expressed in action based on the amount of time you are given to live your life, either to implode or explode, or just fizzle away.

Positive attitudes lead to positive ideas, which lead to positive actions and reactions that create positive atmospheres, which lead to more positive attitudes, which apply to a person, a home, a race, or a nation. The same exact opposite applies to negative attitudes.

This is where the Nemesis Code, (the line, the clock and the cross) clearly and simple explains it, whether you are moving fast or slow, you are moving or being moved in one direction or the other. Your actions are based on your values.

Based on my observations of myself and thousands of people from all over the world, but mainly in America between the two parties, one is intellectual and the other is emotional. People who 'think' are stronger, and tend to enjoy and do better in life than people who just feel their way through life and wear their emotions on their sleeves.

There are two groups of Leftists, the ones that feel sorry for themselves, and the ones that manipulate them. They are trapped in a state of perpetual victim-hood, so consequently someone owes them something and "life" is not fair to them. This ideology flies in the face of the Lord, who said it was, "Better to give than to receive." He also said to follow Him we have to deny ourselves, pick up our cross (burdens) and follow Him. Even J.F.K. said, "Ask not what your country can do for you, but ask what you can do for your country." Leftists refuse to believe that life is primarily what you make of it.

Because of selfishness, bottom-end leftists are easy to control and manipulate; just play with their emotions and they will do anything you want.

Even as I live, this is the plan God gave to me:

1. Start a national revival

2. Reunite the nation to deal with this terrorist threat

3. Give Blacks a chance to take back our dignity, which we sold for a bowl of porridge

4. Do more to put a stop to all of the senseless acts of violence and crime in America, and even to some degree abroad

All of the abortions, rapes, robberies, child abuses and murders are primarily caused by "Lefty Lucy's," who are emotionally unstable and intellectually detached from reality. They would figuratively cut off their own nose to spite their face; this is the sad state of affairs in the nation.

The Pay It Forward System (P.I.F.S.) is not a multilevel or chain letter in the physical sense, it's more like a spiritual net (see details in a Fisherman's Tale); anyway this is the system Jesus used to feed a great multitude with a few loaves and some fish.

Basically it's like this: there are 33 million Black Americans, the vast majority of which (90%) are voting to run from God and hide in darkness and spiritual weakness.

I have made 100 copies of this letter and distributed them to 100 churches. All each pastor has to do is read it, decide whether he believes the truth or not, then if he does, give copies to his elders. Then to the congregation, then give seven copies to seven churches, either in city or out, either in-state or not. If you want to speed up the process, let the congregation help the system. Don't worry; God will be keeping score so everyone will get just what he or she deserves. If each church gives seven and so and so on, the whole nation of Black Americans will either be on board or not. That way we can all decide our own destiny and final resting place, Heaven or Hell.

Let's face it; there is no point in putting money on the table or kicking a dead horse or donkey (jackass). It's hard to steer your race from the back of the nations. Look, this letter is not personal, it's not business, not physical, and not political; it's spiritual, which indeed controls the other four.

Lo and Behold!! You and I have made the Bible come alive, up close and personal. See, the Lord has given us a choice this day, either life and prosperity or death and evil. Jesus said He would separate the sheep on the right and goats on the left, which are you? Or is this like the days of Elijah and the Prophets of Baal? Can you plan, save and set the nation on fire for God or will you follow the plan the Lord gave me? Go ahead and call your God. Louder! Louder! Maybe He's asleep or maybe He's busy.

If we really wish to see some changes in the Black community, then we will have to turn back to God and He will heal our face and our nation.

I hope and pray because of pride, greed, and selfishness you have not hardened your heart against the Lord, as in the days of Egypt, Pharaohs who would not "let the people go." The Lord turned him into a punching bag and a crash test dummy to demonstrate His power to save and to deliver. Who are you, Oh Little Pharaoh to block the way of life from His children, let them decide if they want to go forward or continue to fall backwards out for 33 million, shouldn't there be at least ten million of us not afraid to be Black Americans and go into the future with God and faith, instead of hiding in the past with fear, always crying about being mistreated? The past is dead; let the dead bury the dead.

If God, being the positive force in the universe, says let's move forward into the future where your potential is unfolding, who are you to say, "I vote to go backward?" Can two walk together unless they agree? Then who are you following and whose hands are you holding, walking, and talking to? Tell me, what does light have to do with darkness, or life with death?

Oh Little Pharaoh of all the millions of babies that have been aborted, or millions being born illegitimate, or the millions more who are walking the darkness with broken dysfunctional homes. To all those being killed, robbed, raped, abused, neglected (just in America alone), the vast majority of which is caused by negative, backwards, emotional, weak-minded, leftist thinking and feeling people. The head of the Left controls what the body will do. Crap starts at the top and rolls down hill.

Will the Lord hold you accountable now that you know the truth? Will their blood be on your head? Oh Pharaoh, I hope not for your sake. This is either a declaration of peace or a declaration of war, not with me, but with the One who sent me; the choice if yours.

There are two coats of armor to choose from, the whole armor of God you know, but the whole armor of darkness you may not know:

1. The helmet of damnation

2. The breastplate of unrighteousness

3. Waist belt girded with lies

4. The shield of fear

5. Feet covered with preparation for war

6. And the sword of the dark spirit, the words of weakness (lies)

# ROLL CALL

1. The fear of the Lord is the beginning of understanding.

2. Since God has forgiven you in Christ, if you believe, shouldn't you forgive others as well as yourself?

3. Strength and weakness have this in common, they both respectively create positive and negative attitudes, that lead to actions, that lead to outcomes, that lead to atmospheres, that lead to more attitudes of the same; the two cycles of life. Care to go for a ride?

4. Strong is as strong does, likewise weak is as weak does.

5. Based on the last congressional election, it looks like God is about to start cleaning house, cleaning clocks, and fixing little red wagons, so check yourself before you wreck yourself.

6. Sooner or later, every knee shall bow and every tongue will confess the truth sooner or later.

7. The King of Kings and Lord of Lords is also a master chess player; checkmate in two moves.

8. Good dad/bad dad one is concerned with what we can do and one is concerned with that you can't do. Who's your daddy, anyway?

9. Does it matter to you that our younger generation is/are committing homicide, suicide, and genocide? They are killing each other, themselves and our race. The clock is ticking!

10. Lost Sheep Recovery Department (L.S.R.D.). We get back what the enemy has stolen.

11. Cattle are driven by fear; sheep are lead by faith.

12. This letter may seem harsh, blunt or frank, yet it is only a tiny fraction of the vapors of the cup of the wrath of His indignation.

13. Take it from me; it is a dreadful thing to fall into the hands of the living God; it's going to hurt.

14. I think it would be better if we kept this matter in the family, after all, who wants a news camera in their face asking them, "will you let the people go?"

15. Render to Caesar that which belongs to Caesar, and that which belongs to God to God, or who do you fear more, God or man?

16. The gravity of the depravity of the Left will be the cause of their insanity—which they will suffer for all of eternity.

17. There is a line between the quick and the dead; we just can't see it yet.

18. Young people should always remember that life does not owe you anything; really you owe life for giving you the opportunity to express yourself to be all you can be.

19. If you don't learn from the past, then you are condemned to repeat it. Never allow yourself to be bought or sold, i.e. welfare, section eight, etc.

20. That would be a nice Christmas present for the Lord on His birthday, to have 5-10-15 million presents (lives) to open under His tree (cross)—lives to open up and fill with life, love and power to overcome the world with a spirit of excellence. Some He has not talked to since He formed them in their mother's womb, even since the foundation of the world.

21. The reason for this letter is God's love for you; at least you can't say that no one ever cared enough about you, than to put their own safety in harm's way to tell you the truth. Amen!

22. If you were me, what would you do? Either run the risk of making you angry and hurting your feelings by telling you the truth, or tell you what you want to hear to make you feel good, until you find yourself at the end of the road, suffering for all eternity. What would you do? Where's the love?

23. The Dred Scott decision on July 6, 1854: a group of anti-slavery Whigs and Democrats together with some free-soilers founded the Republican Party at a convention in Jackson, Michigan.

24. According to spiritual history, God created the Republican Party to set the slaves free. He brought our race from Africa. Our ancestors endured cruel hardships and bitter bondage. We have it easy compared to what they went through. He wanted us to keep moving forward, yet we turned our backs on Him. His feelings are hurt and He is offended, yet He would forgive if we turn from dark to light. We now worship false Gods and idols such as, homes, cars, jewels, boats, rims, motorcycles, sex, drugs, etc.

25. Who told you that you were poor? Not God; He thinks you are a priceless, original, living work of art, with His spirit in you.

26. If I had to choose between hurting your feelings or telling you the truth in hopes of saving your soul...well all I can say is have a Kleenex handy, or have a whole box!!

27. No dignity, no shame, know dignity, know shame; no Jesus, no life, know Jesus, know life; no courage, no glory, know courage, know glory.

28. This is a declaration of peace or war, not with me, but with the One who sent me.

29. God did not intend for our race to spend our whole time in America, marching backwards (steppin' and fetchin').

30. If the future holds promise (potential), where would God be more likely to meet you—moving towards the living future or moving towards the dead past?

31. God is a good and Heavenly Father. Before He takes off His belt, He gives us ample time to read the handwriting on the wall, and then He goes to work.

32. Anything or anyone will become unstable, detached from an object or reality if they continue to move to the Left (righty-tighty, lefty-lucy), ten trillion nuts and loose screws can't be wrong.

33. Because of the amount of deception and intensity of this spiritual battle, there is a big shortage of front line solders; the vast majority of saints opt to be proverbial cooks, administrators, medics, mechanics, generals and a boatload of clergy and chaplain corps.

34. My orders are plain and simple: proceed to the front line and don't come back!!

35. It is absolutely, positively mandatory that you must serve in one army or the other, either the army of darkness or the army of light; choose wisely!

36. What does it mean to be born again? It means to see yourself and a life completely 180 degree opposite of the way the world sees you and life, i.e. from worthless to priceless, from backwards to forwards, from weak to strong, from selfish to selfless, from implode to explode, from negative to positive, from death to life, from degenerate to regenerate, from cold to hot, from Hell bound to Heaven bound.

37. Who is God anyway? My best definition is that He is the source essence, force and concept of all life, both animate and inanimate. From the birth of an idea (dream), a baby, a business, a relationship, a nation, a star, the universe, to the death of the same if need be, combined with being the complete base of power, knowledge, and wisdom, merged with incomprehensible love and righteousness wrapped in inexpressible light and perfection, bounding with peace and joy continually.

38. This is the reason we are so very valuable and priceless to Him, because;

a) We are created in His image

b) We are unique; no one in the history of the world was or is exactly like you

c) We have the awesome power to choose life (God), or death (Satan)

39. That's why Jesus had to come to redeem man from death, laying aside His glory. To be less was unthinkable to God.

40. The best way I have found to keep the fire and joy of my salvation burning bright is to keep Jesus as my first love—to love Him more than anything or anyone, because He is the source of life itself.

41. I'm like the little brother that would come to tell you, "Daddy said come home right now Daryl, Lisa, Mabel, Belinda, Joyce, Johnnie, Rick, Denise, Leon, Tracy, Joe, Pat, Karen, Linda, Roy, Barry, Mo, William, Terry, Greg George; Daddy said come home right now!!! Tina, Alice, Sandy, Gene, Chris, Curtis, Kenny, Keith, Rosalyn, Freda, Jimmy, Tony, Candy, Debbie, Betty, Larry, and Steve. Daddy said he's gonna get you!!! Lois, Fred, Rachel, Jackie, Quan, LaShaun, Quita, Ebony, Tasha, Meka, Eric, James, Jamie, Tiffany, and Tlana. He said he's going to get his belt; you'd better hurry up!!! Leonard, Roland, Cassandra, Felicia, Contessa, DeAnna, Alice, Monique, Wendy, Michelle, Michael, Randy, Rochelle, Pam, Beatrice, Jenny, Peter, John, Josh, Joe, Damien, Lucy, Tamika, Cece, BeBe, Phaedra, Jerome, Theodore, Perry, Tabitha, Gena, Darlene, Shirley, Renae, Judy, Donald, Ronald, Constance, Jennifer, Arnez, Lou, Richard, Serena, Benjamin, Carrie, Potter, Poindexter, HJ and, Sara, Mary, Marie, Harold, Breanne, Philip, Benny, Jeffrey, Lee, Secona, Caitlyn—Daddy said you all better get a move on!!!"

Your Little Brother

# A LIVING WORK OF ART (IN PROGRESS)

To P.J. 001 – T.T.O.M.S.L.

I bet you that in less than 1,769 words I could prove, demonstrate, and explain how you are a work of art, if you are willing to learn, believe, and try. What difference would it make in your life? Would it be worth it to you? Your family?

Mark, Set, Go!

It is hard to believe that you and I are living works of art (in progress). I know with so much negativity around us, in people, in our culture, that we even have that same negativity in ourselves—anything from pride to an inferiority complex. Yet the truth is in the hands of a "Master." You are actually an eternal, unique, one of a kind, human being with unlimited potential for goodness.

The problem is that we have been cut off from the course of life (God) that created you through sin (rebellion), yet since we were created in His image, we have an inherent ability to express amazing amounts of positive potential, i.e. science, medicine, music, art, etc.

Yet again since mankind is in a constant state of rebellion against God, in which we can also express mind numbing acts of violence and evil, the very nature and character and spirit of God is love, righteousness and above all, He is Holy, Holy, Holy. He (God) is pure and perfect in all of His ways in thought and word and deed, and what's more He wants us to be like Himself. God is actually life itself. He is the Omnipotent, Omnipresent, Omniscient that holds everything it its place.

But because of the "fall of man," it is utterly, totally, and completely impossible for man to reach out to God; our best work is as a filthy rag to God. Man is in a perpetual state of rebellion, of falling away, going backwards, i.e. Leftism—a degenerative death style.

The nature of sin is death, separation, and weakness. This is the reason God had to send His son Jesus Christ to pay the price for our sin because without the shedding of blood there could be no forgiveness of sin. So by faith in the Lord we can be reunited with the source of life. In case you didn't know, life is positive, but death is negative, and each calls to its own. God wants you to choose Him by submitting to the truth. Satan wants you to choose him by rebelling against the truth.

In order to really understand that you are a work of art in progress, you first must see life according to God's perspective (and if you don't believe that there is a God, then you might as well call Houston because you've got a real problem).

Rule 1: God is the source, force, essence and spirit of life itself; any and all things created—animate or inanimate, physical or spiritual—fall under his jurisdiction. God keeps life in balance by being omnipresent, omnipotent and omniscient.

Rule 2: God's character, His nature, His very being is perfect, pure and above all He is Holy! Holy! Holy! He is the Lord God Almighty!!!

Rule 3: We as man are created in His image, but not with His power. He knows us better than we know ourselves. He knows that because of the "Fall" that we are spiritually dead. He knows that as eternal beings (souls) we are weak, deceitful, sinful, selfish, prideful, lustful, fearful, greedy, apathetic, envious, violent and angry. We all are, to one degree or another.

Rule 4: To the degree (and the sooner) you surrender your life into God's hands, and accept the rules of the game of life, the sooner you will get to the good part of living.

Rule 5: God is a gambling God when it comes to you and His amazing grace. Oh! How sweet the sound. Grace is God's unmerited, undeserving favor towards you. Since God is life, every time you sin it's against Him personally, yet with His grace He is giving you time and opportunity to realize that sin hurts (offends) Him, our fellow man, and we are also hurt. Especially in America, God has shed His grace on thee.

In an abundance, He has given us so much grace that we have become ungrateful, arrogant and foolish, so as to think that we have made ourselves, and are in need of no one, even God.

Most believers don't actually understand that we are saved by grace through faith. It is the gift of God, not of works lest any man should boast. Those Americans who are not saved (Born Again) have no idea how much eternal danger they are in if they die in their sins. Yet most believers don't know what it means to live, learn, and grow in grace. Once you learn to live in grace you will serve the Lord because you want to, not because you have to. That one revelation will set you free from trying to keep the law, thus becoming legalistic—assuming that it's your job and responsibility to save people (which it is not). To grow in grace is to be free to be and accomplish everything God has for you to do in this life. It would be tragic to take grace for granted, because God is not mocked; whatever a man sows that shall he also reap—whether to the flesh which equals death, or to his spirit which equals life.

For those Americans who still have not figured out what all of this means, the reason America is at the forefront (the apex of societal evolution) right now is this: we test mettle all day everyday; we test spiritual mettle to get down to the truth. Without the truth is like being a ship without a rudder. The ship (Nation) would go around in circles or back where it came from. One thing it would not do is go forward in a straight line, so but by the grace of God the Founding Fathers obeyed the truth of God's word, which has brought us to this point. As I said, we test mettle whether in politics, culture, religion, or in a personal capacity. We keep what's right and discard what's wrong. We cling to what's true, and abandon the lies. We keep heading forward and forget looking backwards. We look for a brighter tomorrow and forget a darker past (except to learn from it)—that is up until lately (last 40 years or so). We have a group of so-called Americans who want to enter the arena of ideas, and don't want to have their mettle (ideas) tested by the fire of the truth. They want their 'ways' and 'will' to be accepted, based merely on the fact that they say so. Either they will lie to get their way, or cry and whine to intimidate—until we feel sorry for them, or they become violent. All of which are strains of people that hate God. If you want to come to the table, be prepared to have your mettle tested, okay.

The end game of this message is that God wants you to live a soulful life vs. a soulish life. By the power of your born again spirit, God wants you to embrace His grace and open up your soul to Him, so He can fill it with a life to love what He loves, and to hate what He hates. This is what it means to be set free indeed and to have life more abundantly. When you are free of all of your weaknesses and hang-ups, when those burial clothes are gone into the past, you will be free to have all the positive things that life has in store for only you.

If you live a soulish life you will implode, become self-absorbed, weak, degenerative, hateful, angry, and a vengeful person. If you try to do both, you will be mixed up, confused, lukewarm, a fence straddler, a middle of the roader; you will go around and round in circles and your life will pass you by and then you will die, and then the judgment. Since you actually only go around once, what are you keeping your powder dry for? Your life will be over before you know it.

If you choose to live a soulful life and embrace the truth of God's grace towards you as an American, then you will be able to appreciate all of the blessings He has poured out in this country. It is worth protecting (at all cost) for future generations, when your soul is filled with positivism (God). All of His spirit will dwell with you—all the love, joy and peace you can stand when your soul loves life (God). You will see the beauty in nature, from sunrise to sunset; you will hear music on a deeper level. Food will taste better; even a cold cup of water will be a treat. If you are blessed enough to have a family whose heart (soul) is opened up to God, there will be so many memories of holding hands, smiles, hugs, and kisses and need I even mention that if a husband's and wife's souls love the Lord and each other, there will be passion beyond your ability to comprehend. This is the passionate desire of God's love for you that you should have life at its fullest measure. Your soul is the essence of who you are. Give it to God and He will cause rivers of living water to flow from you, to give to a thirsty and dying world. This is the amazing grace that God has for your soul, my fellow American. Don't bet your soul on a dead horse; the payoff is lousy.

This section is the only one where every word is numbered, because it is the capstone of this book. If you missed grace, then you missed it all. I also suppose that if you missed grace, you will never believe that you are "A Living Work of Art in Progress." I pray to God I'm wrong. I pray by the power of the written word, as the Lord is using these words to paint me, He's painting you. As He's using the truth to sculpt me, He's sculpting you too. As His power is conducting a symphony of my life, He is producing a symphony in you, as well and finally as His love is writing a play of my life, He is writing yours as well.

If there be any life or hope in you, you must admit that you are in God's hands, and as such worth more than a masterpiece or work of art by mere talented men, including Shakespeare, Beethoven, Picasso, or Davinci. Well, I rest my case. Will you believe the truth or the lie? It's your choice. It's your life. It's your destiny. It's your eternity.

- - - - - - - and Stop!

P.S. – Like the truth of God's grace to you, the reason this book comes at you from all different directions, i.e. left/right, inside/outside, fiction/reality, past/present/future, black/white, heart/mind, body/soul, young/old, personally/politically, culturally/religiously, is to show the parallel between the spiritual and physical realms. God's grace is all around you—in front of you to lead you, above you to cover you, behind you to watch your back, beneath you to hold you up, and at your sides to strengthen and support you. The lover of your soul (Jesus) wants you to walk in the truth of His grace, for the salvation of your soul. Amen.

Signed Me[2]

# A FISHERMAN'S TALE

*The Second Greatest Story Ever Told*

Ahoy! Ye swabs draw nigh unto me and I'll tell ye of the adventure of a lifetime. Listen to the words of the Ole Second Mate and bow ye wise thereby…Arrgh!

Once upon a time, called right now, all real men and women went down to the sea (of life) in ships—to test their mettle, to see if they can make the sea of life a better place to sail, and more importantly to make it to the other side, "The Golden Shore," where I hear tell of streets of gold and rivers of living water flowing through, not to mention trees of knowledge and life, a real paradise…Arrgh!

Now there be tell of a captain, Captain Jesus Christ and His ship named "The Cross," is the only one who can take anyone from one shore to the other.

Now lads and lasses, there be some ne'er-do-wells who try to cast off and set sail on their own. They all wind up either in empty relationships, boring jobs they hate, jail, or overly preoccupied with pleasure and entertainment, sports, movies, sex, drinking, parties, or other so-called religions etc. They be either in a perpetual hurricane, stuck going in circles, crashed on jagged rocks, or shipwrecked on a deserted island. Now Old Captain Jesus Christ runs a tight ship. He has two main rules, no going back, and follow orders. The Ole Cap'n has been known to flog, keel haul, or even make some walk the plank, for trying to cause a mutiny or some such foolishness. If you sign on with Him, He demands everything you got, but He gives you everything He's got and He has way more than anything you got or could come close to on your very best day.

Now there be a lot who are even worse than the ones who go to sea on their own and they be the ones who are afraid to leave "Skull Island." They are slackers and sluggards and cowards, not wanting to test their mettle as it were, to see what kind of positive difference they could make in life. There be millions upon millions of them, like so many hermit crabs in a barrel, out of fear of being alone, each one pushing and pulling the one below and above him, back or down.

The really, really sad and tragic truth is that the barrel they are in is actually a pot, and they are being cooked slowly in their own juices (passions), pride, envy, lust, covetousness (selfish), laziness, gluttony (greed), and anger. What's worse, they are killing and eating each other's lives and potential—each one wrapped in a shell of fear, worry, doubt, and all manner of negativity. They spend most of their free time drinking, drugging and fornicating; trying to ignore and numb the pain of the reality of their futile situation.

Now Captain Jesus Christ loves them like He loves us all. He even went down to the pit (Hell), the place where those flames are coming from, and took authority over them so they are actually free to leave the pot by faith in what the Captain did for them. He made a way for them to climb out of the pot, yet some want Ole Captain to climb down into the pit with them. The Cap'n has been there and done that once and for all. He won't do it again. I actually hear tell that some of them set up shop, just like Cap J.C. was in the pot with them, but He's not! Doesn't that beat all! It would be better had they not been born, than to lead those astray, that might have made it out.

Now Cap'n J.C. says that if you sail with Him, He will teach you how to become fishers of men. I hear tell one time, He told His followers where to let down their nets, and they caught so many fish that it strained the nets. Well, like I said earlier, this letter is not a chain letter or a multilevel, it is actually a spiritual net designed to catch men and women. You have a choice to man the nets, get in the nets, or just swim away…here Fishy, Fishy, Fishy, be warned these are shark-infested waters. You may never get a second chance to come aboard.

The Cap'n says there is plenty of work to do. There is a school of some 30 million or so beautiful black bass just waiting to be caught, and there is another 25 to 30 million golden brown walleye out there, plus a ton of red and yellow snapper. Why matie, I even hear of a "Great White Secular Whale," no not Moby Dick, this one's name is Tink-he-slick. No one has been able to get a bead on him, let alone a net, for this one is so self-righteous he thinks he runs the whole show, with no help, not even God's. There are plenty of rewards to be had, here and now, but even more so when we reach "The Golden Shore."

Well maties, what say ye? I told you this was the second greatest story ever told; the first was His, The Captain, The Lord and Savior, Jesus Christ. The second story is that of you; this is your chance of a lifetime, to really live or just go through the motions. The clock is ticking. Will you trust the Cap'n to get you across, will you head out on your own, or will you just stay on Skull Island? Well, we set sail at dawn. Don't worry, we don't shanghai our mates. You must volunteer!

The Second Mate…Arrgh! Thar' She Blows!!

# WHAT'S YOUR FAVORITE DISH?

If you had your choice of a dish of food, what would you like to fill your plate with? There are so many selections to choose from in America, let alone the world—from fish to chicken to steak, not to mention burgers, hot dogs, veal, sausages, vegetables, desserts, cakes, pies, ice cream, or perhaps breakfast foods like pancakes, eggs, bacon, toast, grits, or waffles. Plus, all of the ethnic dishes like Italian, Indian, Thai, Japanese, Mexican, Chinese, French (fries) or my favorite: soul food. Side dishes: corn, peas, rice, cornbread, cabbage, or greens. All types of beans and lentils, plus rolls, potatoes, mac and cheese, not to mention the beverages water, coffee, tea, soda, milk, etc. and that's just to name a few items we can choose to fill our plates with.

In this country it is very easy to overdo it when it comes to our diets. Certain things we eat have been shown to have an adverse affect on our physical health, which left unchecked can cause serious injury or even death. Heart attacks, strokes, high blood pressure, high cholesterol, diabetes, and obesity are just a few of the maladies that can occur if we over-indulge our plates with salt, fat, sugar, etc.

Yet there is another plate that I hear people speak of on different occasions. Have you even heard someone say that they have "a lot on their plate?" This is the spiritual plate we all carry with us everywhere we go, 24/7, and like the physical plate we use to pile food on, the same applies to the spiritual one. Some things we put on our plates are good for us, and some are just as dangerous and deadly as the fat, salt, sugar combination.

The spiritual plate is actually your heart (soul) and if you fill your plate with pride, lust, greed, envy, covetousness (selfish), laziness, and anger you will wind up with a very unhealthy life for sure. You will become a toxic person who will contaminate anyone you come in contact with—on a prolonged basis or sometimes in a brief instant.

Yet on the other hand, there is another diet plan with spiritual food to eat that will bless you and everyone that you come in contact with. These dishes you can eat all you want, and you will only grow bigger and stronger instead of smaller and weaker.

What are these other foods you might ask? They are the fruits of the spirit of God: love, joy, peace, longsuffering, gentleness, goodness, faith, meekness, and self-control. After all, you are what you eat.

*God resists the proud, but gives grace to the humble.*

It has been my observation that one plate is positive and one is negative. The one that is positive tends to lift your spirit, the other that is negative tends to always pull, drag you down, or make you sad, unhappy, just plain apathetic (could care less), or depressed.

Where I live, nine out of ten Americans are obsessed with their own plates. Constantly looking down, eating a plate of food that's making them sick and destroying their one and only precious life. They interact with each other, exchanging one item for another—a little pride for some greed, a little lust for some covetousness, and so-on and so-on. In the end, all you wind up with is the smorgasbord from hell; spiritually dead people eating dead things, but pretending that they are alive, and that dead works can satisfy them. Keep dreaming.

*Pride goeth before a fall.*

No amount of alcohol, drugs, parties, sex, clothes, cars, homes, careers, fame, jewels, motorcycles or even money will be able to make them happy for very long. It's like a dog chasing his tail. If he ever does bite it, it's going to hurt him. So it is with people who indulge in dead works.

This is the reason God had to send his son Jesus Christ to save us from devouring ourselves and each other with "dead food."

The Lord said that those who hunger and thirst after righteousness would be filled. You can't hunger and thirst after righteousness if you are still full of yourself (pride). That's why God will let you pig-out on devil's food until your plate gets so heavy, and you become so weak, that you fall and drop and break your plate (heart). This is all so that you will be able to look up and see how much He loves you.

God would rather we ate high-quality physical and spiritual food, so we can grow big and strong and healthy. Yet because of our pride, we take ourselves through hell and high water before we get it through our thick skulls. It does not matter whether you are an aggressive or passive person. I've seen pride in both. No one wants somebody to tell them how to live or what to eat. Just like little babies, we want our kids to grow up and be mature, but we ourselves don't want to. Go figure.

Well that's the whole enchilada in a nutshell. Don't forget who the real "Big Cheese" is. He's got your best interest at heart, so you can run the race of life to win. You can be a lean, clean, living machine. Do yourself a favor and drop that dead weight plate so Jesus can set you free indeed, that you may have life and life more abundant.

The Dietician

# BATTLE ASSESSMENT

To whom it may concern (Libs): The following is a brief assessment of the battle for America. The reason America is in the condition she is in now, (politically, spiritually and culturally) is because the keepers of the light (truth) back in the sixties were totally unprepared and caught off guard by the "shock and awe" campaign you Liberals launched. Between the two strategies of "divide and conquer," and "surround and suppress your enemy," they really did not stand a chance.

Your campaign was to divide the country politically, racially, socially, sexually, religiously, and patriotically. Tools you used included drug induced separation from reality, and worst of all you divided children from their parents. I don't know if your people knew that by causing so much division and strife, you would surround, isolate and marginalize the vast majority of the Judeo-Christian value system, thereby causing the church to begin a process of internal separation and implosion, which can be seen to this day with all the 600 plus different denominations and doctrines.

The strategy indeed was most effective in establishing a beachhead into the moral fabric of American society, which was the goal all along, because in order to change America you had to change her values from morality to immorality. In all honesty, I admit that you have wreaked havoc on the Black community. The sheer devastation due to the loss of potential alone owed to drugs and violence is catastrophic. That's not to mention the deconstruction of the family and the loss of life.

Be that as it may, I wonder if your planners took into account the tremendous amount of collateral damage, because not only are Black children and families falling in the wilderness, Whites as well as Hispanic families are being consumed with the misery of the futility which is their lives.

You Libs have convinced them to trade their "Dignity for Dollars" and since they don't have the mind to make money without committing a crime, they are hell bent on "getting rich or to die trying." This is the paradise, the utopia, that Liberalism/Socialism has created, which is nothing more than a slave plantation/prisoner of war camp. The sad, ironic and funny thing about it is that since you have turned their minds into mush (emotional) they can't see clear enough to escape the trap, which means they are not that upwardly mobile, which means they can't really help you a whole lot because they have to wait to be told what to do, how to think, and feel, which when you're in a battle is a big disadvantage if your troops can't think for themselves—therefore defeating the goal of Socialism in the first place (catch-22).

I will say that you Libs have done a lot of potential damage to our young kids in the dumbing-down/sexing-up process. The reason I say it is still potential is because they are still young and there is time for them to change their minds.

In my opinion your plan was aggressive, fanatical, and strategic, but grossly short sighted, ill advised and poorly executed. After all, only 40 years into your campaign your party is running out of steam. That's why you are losing elections and you don't have anymore unverifiable lies to tell, plus, all the effects of the lies you told in the 60's are coming home to roost (cluck-cluck).

Even though you had the church reeling on its heels for almost 40 years, you guys forgot to read the part of the Bible that says after 40 years God hits the reset button, thereby giving people a chance to correct a left turn into a right turn (like Michael Medved said).

I also believe, if this was any other country in the world that you would have succeeded in your endeavors, yet there is one small fact that you forgot to calculate into your plans, and that is "whose house is this?" America is God's house, even with all of the hate and corruption that the Liberals generate, propagate and instigate. God's spirit still dwells here more than any other place in the world, bar none.

That's part of the reason why caring what the world thinks of us is a joke you guys on the Left like to tell, but we are not amused.

I suppose since you don't actually believe in the kingdom of light that you don't believe in the kingdom of darkness either. What a pity, because they both believe in you.

Oh and by the way Libs, we know you are hoping to use felons and illegals in 2008. Hopefully the President has enough strength to pass a law requiring voter I.D. so there will be no cheating on either side of the aisle.

Now in regards to the "battle," since the church has finally stopped reeling from your assault, although their backs are against the wall, the 40 year reset is about to occur, and since God usually sends a teacher or a prophet around this time like M.L.K., I wonder who it will be this time?

From now on Libs, there will be no more walks through the park with the help of our allies in talk radio, you will have to fight for and earn every inch of American soil and most of all every life (soul).

The heat is about to be turned-up one million degrees hotter than the sun. May the best kingdom win. Good luck, 'cause you're going to need it. You Libs hit like girls. Now that it's our turn to save all the people on the spiritual plantations/P.O.W. camps, it would be a good time to start thinking for yourself—to stop following your parents and grandparents, "just because." This also would be a good time to forgive people for past sins and self imposed slavery, to stop being envious of what other people have, and to learn to be thankful for the life God gave you. You have more potential than you realize with His love in you.

# BREAKING BREAD

Even though I can no longer turn to the Left (backwards counterclockwise, cold, subtracting, lefty-lucy-unstable) my heart and mind are with the Black church that remains on the Left in darkness. The Libs are in deep, deep denial (like the river in Egypt). You will never ever get them to step back and see themselves for what they are. Nevertheless, I have seriously thought about the Black churches' dilemma of not wanting to leave family, friends and political tradition in view of this. Here is my solution to the problem.

I know for a fact that God does not condone car-jacking, yet I'm inclined to believe that he does not have a problem with a political party jacking for a worthy cause. Like the saying goes, one good "jacking" deserves another. The Democrats are not the Democrats of old, who I genuinely believe did have the best interest of the poor and working class man in mind. The Liberal Democrats of today came to power during the political, religious, cultural, sexual and drug revolutions of the sixties, not to mention the suspicious and untimely assassinations of M.L.K. and J.F.K. so don't feel bad about breaking ties with people and a movement that don't have your best interest at heart. These people are only interested in gaining power at any expense. If you take an honest (?!) look back to 40 years ago, at least we had hope for the future. Now 40 years later with the "Dems," there is nothing but hopelessness and a lot of "talk." The proof of this fact is witnessed in our children, who are our future. The vast majority of them have joined the "hip-hop nation" which is controlled by weakness and darkness. They are being led by a group of "pied pipers" to drown in a lake of fire.

As the Lord has not left or forsaken me, nor will I them. If we are children of God then we must wage full scale, spiritual, political and cultural war against anything and everything that would seek to destroy our future. Liberalism and Socialism are the right and left hands of Satan in America.

I thought I heard the Bible say that you were the head and not the tail (Deuteronomy 28:13); that you were above and not beneath?

Well I'm from Missouri (show-me).

From the place where I'm standing, as I look down on the situation (being seated in the heavens) there are three options that you have to choose from.

1) You can continue to play around by continuing to follow the spiritually blind. Will you not go blind and fall into a ditch yourself? Isn't that what your father told you would happen if you play with yourself—go blind (to the truth)?

2) Jump ship (which is what I had to do). Righty-tighty. The more I move to the right, the more respectful, thankful, independent, unselfishly generous, disciplined and responsible I become. Everything that moves to the right both spiritually and physically is positive, clockwise moving forward in time, thereby gaining additional strength both spiritually, physically and financially. According to statistics, 90% of Blacks vote Democrat. They say if 20% to 25% of Blacks would vote conservative, then the Liberal Democratic Party would stop dead in its tracks. That's not a bad scenario, but I can go one better.

3) Jack the party. This is the best option in my opinion, for in doing so you would kill three birds with one stone:

i.) We would begin the process of reclaiming our dignity that we so foolishly sold to the Libs in the form of entitlement and welfare programs for a measly few trillion dollars. Our dignity, as a race and individually, is the most priceless attribute we possess. Without it you will have no honor, valor or virtue. You will have diminished self-respect, worth, and confidence, with no real hope of regaining faith and truth. I could go on and on, so let it suffice to say that the kingdom of God is rooted in dignity and honor, so to not have dignity would probably line you up for the other kingdom.

ii.) The second benefit for jackin' the party is for the country. In one fell swoop you could unite the country, in that both parties would want what is best for the nation. No more pity party!! No more pity party!! No more pity party!!! No more of a party that tries to induce self-pity in its subordinates, to make them weak, jealous, fearful, angry, vengeful, unforgiving, lustful, violent, lazy and ungrateful. Instead of finding ways to be grateful (positive) about the life they have, that God has given them, they have been programmed to be negative. No more setting a bad example for our kids in our words and actions, no more getting in bed with immoral people. No more doing the same thing over and over and expecting different results (insanity). No more being like a dog chasing his tail "stuck on stupid." If we stand strong and be of good courage, like the Lord told His children when entering the Promised Land flowing with milk and honey, this would be found pleasing in our God and our country.

Can you see a nationwide revival sweeping across the land with the Lord pouring out His spirit in abundance?

Can you see demanding excellence from our kids again as we lead by example?

Can you see economic boom with people starting to save and invest more of their money on themselves and their kids' future instead of things they don't need, can't afford or are bad for their health?

Can you see a clean and peaceful neighborhood to live in, and can you also say "Cultural American renaissance," which includes an outpouring of positivism, as there would be a rebirth of music, poetry, art, dance, books, plays and theater?

Can you say "Political harmony," as the Left and Right could provoke each other to good works? America is going to need all her strength to face these radical people who do not like our God, our people, or our way of Life. We will need unity so that we may stand.

iii.) The third thing we have to gain is that I'm sure if we were to turn our hearts back to God as a nation, He would forgive, cleanse and heal our hearts and land. I'm sure He would be pleased.

Well that's my solution to the problem on the Left. Now whatch-ya'll wanna-do? I got them ski-masks and them "thangs" in the trunk (figuratively speaking), so are you down to ride? Do you want to talk about it or be about it?

If it should come to pass that you run into stiff opposition from the hard core leftist, here are a few things to keep in mind. Hard core Libs are paranoid schizophrenics with suicidal tendencies. They are experts at projecting their fears, weaknesses and hate onto other people—i.e. such as how they make Blacks fear and hate Republicans in order to keep them on plantations, or how they are split between what God created them to be and how they feel, or how in the Clinton administration they were too afraid to deal with the terrorists. They think appeasing evil will make it go away. They are so fearful of progress that they want to live in the past, like they re-enslaved the Black race. The way they treat criminal or the terrorist activity indicates that they have a death wish. Because of the mental and emotional pain they suffer on a daily basis, they hate pain, suffering and tribulation for themselves or anyone else. This is why they seek to pacify everyone with money or resources. Pain and suffering are a part of life, and we all must experience it to some degree or another. In God's kingdom, He uses pain, suffering and tribulations to wean you off of weakness, to purify you and free you, and to make you more like Him (strong).

In Satan's kingdom, he uses the same to wean you off of strength, to poison you and enslave you, to make you more like him (weak).

By not allowing Blacks to fight and struggle on our own, we are deprived of the victory gained from winning our own battles—the sense of self worth derived from doing a thing yourself; the outpouring of God's own grace for doing His will. Now most of us have to wait on a check to do anything. Dignity for dollars. What a rip.

The Bible says that God chose the poor to be rich in faith (James 2:5). This means that God has so much confidence in Himself that He knows what He has is better than money. He knows money can't buy love, make you whole, or get you into Heaven. This is why God does not pity you. He has compassion, He has mercy, and most of all He has grace for you to use while you have a chance. Since you are created in His image, He knows what you are capable of. To pity you would be to pity Himself, and He is not pitiful. To be pitiful means you are too weak and dumb to help yourself, which for you is a lie; lazy maybe, but not weak.

If He was going to pity any of us, He would pity our distant relatives over in Africa that are dying of disease and starvation at a phenomenal rate. So for all you thugs that are hoping that there is Heaven for a "G," you had better think again. When you plant a seed for a tree, apple, orange or pear, you dig a hole in the dirt, then with water and sunlight a tree blossoms and brings forth fruit. The entire hip-hop nation is digging a hole in spiritual dirt. How far are they going to dig?

Saying that you don't need the truth or the Lord in your life is the same as saying you don't even know enough to know that you need the Lord in your life, since every breath you take is in His hands. The Libs would like you to treat them as gods. In order to feel important, the Libs need to rule over you. Since you believe you are poor and needy, they will keep defending you as long as they can keep you poor and needy. This makes them feel needed and important. If you think I'm lying, just leave the party and watch them go nuts.

# FEEDING THE DRILL

Since we are both physical and spiritual beings, which means for there to be real, meaningful, and positive help provided, both sides of our being must be addressed. Addressing the spiritual side means learning to be optimistic, grateful, and determined to make a good life for yourself, whether rich or poor (upwardness).

On the other hand, when you address the physical side first (e.g. throwing money at a situation) if the person (people) are negative, ungrateful, with no determination to make a good life for themselves, then no amount of money will make them happy. You can't buy happiness; it comes from within (Godly self respect).

When middle class White, Black and Brown Democrats continue to feed money into the Liberal Socialist movement, the money goes in, then goes up to the top, then straight down to the bottom (with few exceptions). This "feeding the drill" effect will give those at the bottom a means to not only grow larger, but with every generation to dig deeper into futility, which will require more and more money to sustain, which will eventually tax the middle class into the same boat as the people they tried to help. The truth and tough love may not feel good at first, but it always works in the end.

# BREAKING BREAD/GOING OLD TESTAMENT

If it should come to pass that a young person from 20 or so should have the fire of the Lord shut-up in his bones, and is tired of seeing his generation get wiped-out before his eyes, or for the most part trapped in a demoralized weak, poor, and violent lifestyle, then let that person clean his hands, mind, heart, and body for the work of the Lord. Since the Lord is the truth and the truth is the spiritual "bread" of life, then by all means you can take this truth, give thanks for it, break it, and give it to all those people who love God and want to save America; those who are hungry for the truth in their lives, who want to create a culture of excellence for themselves and their kids, whether rich or poor, black, white, brown, red, or yellow, male or female, who would like to see some real love, joy and peace in the only life they will ever have.

People: believe the truth "that life is what you make it" and "with God all things are possible."

You, being a young person, will have many years to give to the Lord's work to save as many souls as possible. I believe that there are books in Heaven being written for people who actually stand-up for the truth, those who make a real difference in their society.

If you continue to break the bread of life (Jesus) in the blue states, you may very well bring the plantations back to life where people would value each other more than things or money. There is a tremendous amount of work to do. A little help, please. The best way to keep the Devil off of your tail is to stay on his. I say this because there will be opposition to your mission. There are groups (Tribes) who will try to stop you or sabotage your work. The slave master-ites, the house Negro-ites, the Aunt Jemima-ites, the Uncle Tom-ites, and the step-n-fetch-ites are all around you. If they do not wish to help save the country then let them be, for they will learn the hard way about fighting against God.

Then will it not be as in the days of the Old Testament, when Elijah the Tishbite gathered all the worshipers of Baal and himself to see who was chosen by God. They had spent some 40 years whoopin' and hollerin' to the god they serve, only to watch the plantations sink further into the abyss. Then you, in only a few short months, will be well on your way to saving your race, your country, and being a blessing to God Himself. Is there a Joshua in the house?

# IS THERE A DOCTOR IN THE HOUSE?

Take your pick. Would you rather be the doctor or the patient? Let's just say you are the doctor and a victim ("vic") comes to the O.R. with two wounds—gunshot wound to the chest and a stab wound to the leg. Which wound would you treat first? The life threatening one of course. Well that's the exact same scenario that is playing out between the "Libs" and "Cons" (Conservatives), in that the Democrats keep harping about a culture of corruption on the Right, when due to the immorality promoted by the Left, they are what is killing the nation. They have created a culture of implosion and of destruction that is destroying the nation from the inside out.

The knife wound of the "Rep" can be healed by throwing anyone caught with their hand in the cookie jar in jail. But if we erode the moral fiber of the nation, we will actually create a culture of corruption, which we claim not to want. Ok, your turn to be the vic.

# WHO LOVES YOU BABY?

What we have here, is a failure to communicate, all the across the board. The men can't communicate with the women and vice versa. The young have lost touch with the old and vice versa. The "Cons" and the "Libs" fight all day long. There seems to be a great divide between the rich and the poor. The weak are at war with the strong and vice versa. Lord knows the Blacks and Whites have issues.

In my opinion, based on 40 years of observation and experimentation, the reason for so much confusion and dissension is all because of a big misunderstanding, whether by ignorance or deception or rebellion, mankind has forgotten where he came from. For those believing the truth, know we were created by God. For those believing lies, think we evolve from some pond scum or some such nonsense. If that were true we would not have a need for a conscious (to be aware of self and right and wrong) we would be like any other wild animal acting on pure instinct. I don't see monkeys or dogs or birds building ships, planes, buildings, going into space, writing love songs or poetry, making movies, or building a civilized civilization. (Sometimes I wonder about that.)

For those of you who wish to continue to believe lies, unless you change your mind there is no hope for you, there is no need for you to read anymore, you will learn the grave error of your decision at the end of your journey.

The great football game of life is playing out right before our eyes. We who believe the truth have a goal to make it to Heaven. Those who believe lies are trying to make it to hell. Our job is to turn as many of them as we can to go with us. Their job is not really to stop us, just to keep acting like they can't figure out the difference between right and wrong. Since God gave us all who are not severely mentally ill a conscience, we know right from wrong. Based on the "Golden Rule," do unto others as you would have them do unto you. It is as simple as that. If you don't want anyone lying, stealing, killing, cheating, aborting, lusting, enslaving, etc., then you don't do it to anyone else. It is true. You can't cheat an honest man.

If you want to know the truth, the real you of you is your consciousness. In other words, you are the little weak person who knows he/she is doing wrong and is not strong enough to help himself. There are spiritual forces that are heavily invested in your demise. In other words, all you so called gangsters, thugs, and hoods, that's not the real you "acting out." If you get caught slipping and are sent to the other side, when you come face to face with the truth, those dark forces will not be with you acting tough, and it will be just that little person who was afraid to be honest with yourself, but who knew better. But at that point, it will be too late because the real big boys play for keeps; there is no coming back for a do-over. This life is temporary; 70-90 years or so. The other side is forever. Think about it. Some of your people need to tap your brakes and make a u-turn. Some need to lock 'em-up and do a 180. Others need to hit the brakes and throw it in reverse. You are too close to the edge. Don't drive your only life over the cliff of defeat. You need to treat yourself not defeat yourself. You feel me?

The reason why life is so hard to understand is because we are all born twisted, in that our conscious is wrapped in self pity and pride (like a candy cane). These are the sources of all man's reasons for a failure to communicate with God, himself, and his fellow man. This is the definition of weakness. The reason for our dilemma is all boiled down to our inability and unwillingness to communicate with God. For those that seek Him must do so in spirit and truth. To do this means that you believe He exists (truth). In spirit means you have no regard for this life, in respect for the defense of the truth for the benefit of your fellow man. Because the truth will out live man on this earth. If you are in the truth, then eternal life is in you. If you lay your life down for His sake, he will pick it back up for you on the other side. Testing time.

Again I ask the question, who loves you baby? God does. He loves you so much. He wants you to be just like Him. After all, if you believe the truth then He is where you came from, right? Nevertheless He loves you so much He wants you to make up your own mind based on your life. He gave you the awesome gift, power, and privilege to choose to be like Him or the other fellow.

God is full of and is the essence of life, power, joy, honor, peace, prosperity, faith, hope, etc. He is the authority of everything that's good. He is pure light, truth, and righteousness. He wants us to be whole (one) as He is. Because if that were the case there would be no need for all the misunderstanding and miscommunication we see in this generation.

If we allowed the Lord to unwrap us from all of our pride and self-pity, then we would be weaned off of weakness. God's love would equal power to overcome this life. The truly strong would teach the weak. There would be a cascade of evolving benefits to America; more than I could mention, for example, Honor if we honored ourselves—no drugs, alcohol, cigarettes, crime, sexual immorality, and then health issues would decrease dramatically. With an atmosphere of positivism and excellence our families would be healed or kids would strive to be the best they could be. Since no man is an island unto himself, we would have a positive effect on our neighbors and co-workers. What if they were more motivated than you? There would be no need to worry about age, color, sex and social status. We'd have men respecting woman again, and woman respecting themselves. God's truth would give you the power to be what He called you to be—house maker, ditch digger, or rocket scientist. There would be no need to be jealous of the rich because money won't get you into Heaven. In some cases, it will actually keep you out. Enjoy the truth and the world could not contain the books that could be written about man's unused potential. The power to walk on water is hidden in man.

## THE SPIRITUAL MATRIX

If God can get you to unwrap yourself from yourself, then you can see which way the world really does turn (left or right). That is why He sent His wonderful, beautiful, mighty son Jesus to teach us to be like Him—not like Mike. My job is to try and get you unplugged from the spiritual matrix, like the movie, so you can see what's worth living for and what's not.

If you have been paying attention, then you should be unplugged. What you do next is up to you. When you become like Neo then all the attacks of weakness will be of no effect to you. When you find yourself in God, you will have overcome this world. You will be like the Apostle Paul. No manner of things, neither death nor principalities, nor powers, nor things present, nor things to come, nor height, nor depth, nor any other created thing shall be able to separate us from the love of God, which is in Christ Jesus our Lord.

If you want to live a life of mediocrity, watching T.V., going to clubs and parties, then keep doing what you're doing and keep getting what you're getting—but you're missing out.

# THE FINEST THINGS MONEY CAN'T BUY

God's love in your life equals power in your life to overcome all of your weaknesses. If you are really, really serious about following Him, then your family can have his love, respect, peace and joy which will make your home like Heaven on Earth.

*If a husband and wife are bending over backwards to please each other, then how can they bump heads?*

The Bible says if you train up kids in the way they should go, then when they are older they will not depart from the truth (Proverbs 22:6), so the sooner you get started the better, ok?

The truth is two faced. On the one hand it is the hardest force in the universe (1 + 1 = 2), and on the other hand it is the softest force in the universe (e.g. the trusting heart of a child). That's why Jesus is known as a lion and a lamb. On the one hand He is as strong as He can be, and on the other He is meek as can be.

The truth is in the mystery of marriage, of man and woman in the truth. When the man learns to let go of his weakness and stand strong for the truth, and when the woman learns to surrender to the truth, then intimacy will cause the two to become one flesh. Every touch, every look, every aroma, will be magnified in slow motion. You will probably have to invest in sound proof walls for the bedroom. You feel me? No more gossiping with girlfriends. No more staying out with the fella's. It's about going home to be with your mate and kids, because who you are is in them (family) not in those strangers. This is God's love for you. So I ask you, who loves you baby? Jesus does.

# BLACK HISTORY MONTH

The thing that Black Americans have to do is take a step back and look at the big picture. On the one hand, you have a very few incidents of reported discrimination from "Whites" on the Right. There is an almost complete lock-down (90%) of Blacks on the Left being told by "Whites" what to think, how to feel, and act and vote out of fear of the "right".

I would much rather face a few reported incidents of racism on an individual basis than submit my will to a bunch of snobs who happen to be White. To me, it not only looks like real modern slavery, it also shows how weak and un-unified our race has become from depending on others to fight our battles for ourselves.

If Blacks would become Americans, not disenfranchised victims, and learn about politics, the judicial system, and the constitution there would be no need for anyone to watch over us.

I think it is an offense and an insult to depend on Liberal Democrats to speak for the Black race in America. I have the utmost respect for past leaders of the civil servants from Harriet Tubman, Medgar Evers, Rosa Parks, and Martin Luther King Jr. I think it is time for some new Black history to occur in this country. We need to be able to look back 40 years from now and let our kids and their kids see that we have their best interest at heart. Love is a sacrifice. Is there a Moses in the house? Our courtship with the Liberal Democrats began about 80 years ago. We have been going downhill ever since, even to this very day. The way you can tell we are headed down hill is to look at our youth. They are becoming weaker and weaker. Fortunately for us, after every generation (40 years) God allows for a wake-up call (so to speak); for those that are looking for answers to find a way to a better life. Forty years ago Martin Luther King Jr. was the one who stepped up to the plate. We are now approaching another 40 year cycle. We as a race cannot afford to do another bid with the Dems. That is if we love our kids and their kids and so on.

History is unfolding right before your eyes and ears. The only problem is that it's not worth talking about because of the negativity of the spiral descent into insanity. Almost everyone is turning a deaf ear and a blind eye as our youth are hell bent on self destruction. No one out of all the parents, teachers, politicians, and religious leaders seem to have a voice loud enough to be heard. Hello, a little help please.

## PART III

An illusion of an illusion, an analogy of an analogy, an allegory of an allegory of truth, life and freedom vs. lies, death, and slavery—this section of my book uses visual spiritual images to draw out the truth in comparison to the lies. I did not intend to write a 3$^{rd}$ part to the book; it kinda' wrote itself.

This is my version of a spiritual preemptive strike to avoid Civil War II.

# EXTRA EXTRA

Read all about it. The greatest disaster combined with death and destruction unequaled in American history, cannot hold a candle to this monster. One of the strangest things about this catastrophe is that for the most part it has gone unreported to the masses. Go figure! And in some circles it was reported that it was celebrated. You may ask what is this disaster that has caused so much destruction and misery that has gone largely unreported to the masses? Before I tell you, there is one thing you must understand and that is that the physical realm is an extension of the spiritual realm.

Everything you see that is man made had to exist in someone's mind. That's the place where the spiritual and the physical realm meet, which gives man the power to create. Well likewise before God created the Heavens, the Earth, and all living things, they existed in his mind. So, as in reference to natural disasters there are spiritual disasters as well. And this is the catastrophic event I am referring to—a spiritual hurricane.

I know that the vast majority of Americans would never place the condition of our nation in the context of a hurricane, yet as you will soon see the analogy is identical down to the letter. Before we go into the eye of the storm, there are a couple of rules and points to remember.

The first and most important thing you need to learn is that in the entire universe, and especially here on Earth, including the human experience, is that there are only two forces that shape, control, and govern the universe. They are strength and weakness. Now these two forces manifest themselves in different capacities such as positive vs. negative, right vs. wrong, lawful vs. unlawful, moral vs. immoral, hot vs. cold, intellect vs. emotions, masculine vs. feminine, free vs. slave, light vs. dark, truth vs. lies, love vs. hate, spirit vs. flesh, life vs. death, intelligent vs. ignorant, hard vs. soft, good vs. evil, God vs. Satan. These are a few examples of the two forces in opposition to each other. Just in case you missed it, the vast majority of people in America and the world believe that

Satan is some great, strong, powerful enemy of God and man, when in actuality he is the expressed image and the epitome of weakness. He is the complete 180 degree opposite of God. So what this means is it is not about how strong he is, but about how weak your mind is. The power of weakness is in lies and ignorance. People give him way too much credit as to conceal the weakness that is resident in all of us; the very same weakness that pulls us down to do things that are harmful to ourselves and our fellow man. The definition of weakness is any thought, ideology (spirit) feeling, action, person, or movement that would cause you to turn against God, yourself, or your fellow man. The two types of people who show more weakness and evil in the world are the self absorbed (full of pride) and the ones full of self pity (those that for whatever reason are ignorant of their own potential). The battle of strength and weakness in humanity and in us goes like this. Strength usually pities weakness. Weakness uses that pity to gain advantage over strength, "a little leaven, leavens the whole lump."

Now that we have had a small glimpse at the ruler, kingdom, and subjects of weakness (darkness) it stands to reason that the direct opposite is the kingdom of light; this is God's kingdom where truth, love, strength, and freedom dwell. The only way to enter and be a part of this kingdom is to accept God's plan of salvation in His only begotten son Jesus Christ. Then if you are like most of us, you will begin a long, painful, bitter sweet process of being weaned off of weakness. Depending on how much you realize your need to be saved, will determine how hard your struggle with weakness will be. The number one reason we struggle with weakness (sin) so much is because of pride. No one wants to give up control of their life to anyone even if the weakness in your life will cause you to live an inferior quality of life as opposed to a victorious life in Jesus. The second and third reason we struggle so hard is because of lies and ignorance. When you braid a cord of pride, lies, and ignorance it is not easily broken, and in fact that cord is "weak" enough to keep a person trapped in darkness their entire life. Nowhere else is this witnessed so clearly as in people who go to church for all their lives and still struggle with weakness, or even worse they cast their lots (votes) with people who hate God, and still think they are serving Him, like the people who crucified the Lord and killed His disciples thought they were doing the will of God.

We all fall short and get weak sometimes but that should be the exception not the rule. We are not perfect, so we will say or do something wrong at times but God is forgiving and will forgive you if you ask Him. But to live in willful sin and think because you feel sorry for yourself (self pity) when He has the power to set you free, that He has to accept you and your service to Him (the Cain and Able complex). All I can say is that you are taking an awfully big risk. What's the use of running the race only to be disqualified at the end of it (your life)?

The biggest spiritual obstacle that blocks and hinders your walk with God is unforgiveness. The whole kingdom of God, as it pertains to us, is based on the fact that through His son God forgave us. So for you or me to hold a grudge against a person or a race of people puts your relationship with God on eggshells, "so step lightly." Whatever is loosed is loosed. Whatever is bound is bound. On earth as it is in Heaven.

Now having said all that, before we get down to the business of tracking hurricanes (spiritual ones), you need to understand the number 40 in relation to the spiritual realm. As briefly touched on before, the number 40 signifies the end of one thing and the beginning of another or vice versa. This is seen in the Bible when the children of Israel ticked God off after he brought them out of Egypt and bondage. He let them wander in the desert for 40 years before they went into the "Promised Land" (Numbers 32:13). Then there was the flood of Noah's day—it rained for 40 days and nights. Also when Jesus began his ministry, he fasted in the wilderness for 40 days. Forty is a very powerful number. The reason the number 40 is so very important to us today is because it has been just about 40 years since hurricane Liberalena (L.L.) turned from a spiritual depression to a full fledged hurricane and slammed into the U.S. with a vengeance. That is unparalleled. The amount of spiritual and physical damage and destruction cannot be calculated in a thousand years, so many lives, hopes, and dreams were completely and utterly wiped off the face of the earth.

I don't think it is a coincidence that we've recently experienced the worst hurricane season in history (2006). Personally I think it is to draw attention to the truth. As I said "40" means either the end or the beginning of a thing; the "choice" is ours. In order for you to understand how a spiritual hurricane works, I will attempt to reconstruct the operation, power and goal of one. The core (heart) of L.L. is based in the lie that the government has the right, power, or responsibility to care for its citizens from the cradle to the grave. Only God can and should do that. This lie is precipitated by pride (self-absorption), unwillingness to submit to God's authority, mixed with ignorance of the truth of the consequences that will arise automatically when you disobey God's word. These three are the components that give L.L. life, or in this case death.

Before I forget, when the Liberal Democrats launched the sexual drug, cultural, religious revolution of the 60's is exactly when L.L. got started. Since L.L. is founded in weakness that is what she feeds on. She must continually create an atmosphere of negativity, fear, pride, hate, lies, lust, violence, slothfulness, anger, indifference, rebelliousness, unforgiveness, etc. This is the weakness that "burns" (lives) in the hearts and minds of the people who ascribe to the Liberal ideology.

Just for the record I have rated L.L. a category 40, as the height of her surge wall is 40 feet. Her speed range is 2,500-6000 miles per second. It is crucial to understand that since L.L. is on the Left, her cyclone spins to the Left, as in counter clockwise. That's why they are obsessed with the past and they hate positive progress. They are very cynical about the future because L.L. cannot be fed or grow on anything positive, and since she is intelligent she has objects of attack that her surge wall slams into trying to destroy so she can feed and grow stronger. The four things are God, family, constitution, and morality. These are the foundational pillars of America that keep the nation free and strong, no matter how you look at it.

Horizontally or vertically, as if on a number line, they would be in negative numbers, always trying to subtract from life. If vertical, as in a thermometer, they would drop below freezing. This is why the country has become so cold (road rage, increased crime, etc.). And that is why as a Black man in America, I have considerable indignation at the "Lib Dems," for they have turned my race into their main source of food. This happened in the '60s when they flooded my people with entitlement programs which eventually took away our motivation and desire to move ahead positively into the future. The damage is so severe for so long, that we as a race are moving backwards in time. That is why we have created our own sub-culture. America is moving to the right into the future, and we are left behind. That is why there is so much Black-on-Black crime, broken homes, unwed mothers, drug, and alcohol and health abuse. Ninety percent of Blacks vote Democratic because they give them "free" money in exchange for our dignity.

We have moved so far back in time, we are now in the new slavery complete with slave masters, plantations, crops, Aunt Jemimas, house Negroes, Uncle Toms and slave traders. Can you guess who's who? As I said earlier, this is what happens when a 40 foot wall of pure weakness slams into a man, woman or child, and makes contact with the weakness and ignorance that's in all of us. A person can be swept up with a life filled with pain, heartache, and suffering until the day they die, or live a life of apathy or mediocrity, while some are snatched out of their mother's womb and killed. So much wasted potential. I have seen kids six, seven and eight years old with great minds and hearts, then ten years later they are pregnant, in jail, on drugs and alcohol doing crimes, etc.— just wasting their lives over nothing. That first drink or puff or sexual encounter or crime, and you go from having a destiny of greatness to waiting for your fate.

L.L. is full of hate and vengeance. "Like you know who," Libs seem to live to hate and hate to live. Back in the '60s when they said do what you _feel_ and if it _feels_ good, do it. What if what you feel like doing causes other people harm or brings down society? What if what feels good will make you feel bad in the long run? Do you think they knew what they were doing back then? I wonder. I wonder if H.C., who is the eye of the storm, would put a stop to L.L. if she read this? I wonder? Hmm.

# HOW TO BUILD A BETTER LEVY

I never knew there were so many different conservative factions; neo-cons, fiscal-cons, judicial cons, religious-cons and counting me as of 2004 about five Black conservatives. Even though I'm surrounded by a sea of blue, it feels so good to be out from under the head of people who are afraid to use their whole mind. They just live in their feelings and emotions, whether they are negative or weak or wrong. "If it feels good, do it" or just do what you feel.

Anyway, fellow conservatives, you may have never considered it before, just as L.L. is a spiritual hurricane, you guys are a spiritual levy. If it were not for you holding L.L. back, she would have done even more damage than she has already. So you guys and gals should give yourselves a hand. As much as I love America and my race, it feels good to know where my enemy is. Finally, it took me a long time to see the light. Now I can't wait for the rest, or as many that will believe the truth, to have the courage to leave the plantation.

I have to admit you guys had me kinda' worried when you stood up against the President over his first judicial nominee, Ms. Miers. I thought you guys would fragment the levy and give L.L. some weakness to feed on. Thank God the President regrouped and appointed a strict constitutionalist, Justice Sam Alito, with '08 around the corner. That was a risky move. Even though L.L. is weakening, she is still dangerous. She is off in the Gulf looking for some weakness to feed on. I am glad that you guys have a "pair" to stand up to Mr. Bush because of how important this Justice is to the salvation of this nation. Now if we could just get the Reps in D.C. to get a pair, we could make some real progress in remaking the nation whole again.

Don't underestimate the power of weakness; it took 30 years to build the "con levy." If we are not careful, L.L. could knock you back about ten years into the past, even in her weak state. She's just waiting for a worst case scenario to blame the Reps. You can see the attacks that they are bringing against the White House, trying to feed her. We should make moves to fix the borders, Bird

Flu, illegal aliens, and the war in Iraq so as to keep "the eye" from having a solid platform in 2008.

Also, I think we should support the President even more—after all he has taken the brunt of L.L. for five years, with winds of weakness of up to 6,000 miles per second attacking him from head to toe. Most people could not stand that much negativity, so cut him some slack.

The other thing that we need to do is drive a wedge between L.L. and her favorite food source, Black Americans. We all see almost everyday those Aunt Jemimas, house Negroes and Uncle Toms going around "ginning-up" anger, self-pity, frustration, and sorrow in my race to feed L.L. I will be so glad to put a stop to them. Talk about being "stuck on stupid," I'm tired of them playing on my people's hurt and wounded feelings just to make money and feed L.L. They have no solutions or answers; they just point the finger of blame to keep people from looking at them. That is why I wrote this book. If we can hold the line for a few more years and keep the House and Senate, and bring conservatives to the Supreme Court, then L.L. will slow down to less than 1,000 mps. People will be able to see L.L. for what she really is, a hideous monster that preys on the misery of emotionally weak-minded people.

The best thing we can do is to tell the truth and let God do the rest. This chapter might do the trick. To be detoxified off of spiritual weakness can be long and painful, depending on how bad the addiction is. I personally would rather hurt someone's feelings, if it would save their soul. I would hope someone would do the same for me. That is why it is so important for this "Human Levy" not to fail. So fellow conservatives, hold the line for the sake of America no matter what. If your hands bleed (spiritually speaking), your back aches or you sweat bullets, even until every muscle in your body is strained, whatever you do, hold the line. The future of your offspring is at stake. Just something to think about at the dinner table.

## MALE HURRICANE BORN

Wait a minute! This just in. Early reports indicate a spiritual inspiration forming somewhere over America—thick clouds, thunder, lightning, winds gusting up to 1,000 mps, heavy rains. The winds moving to the right (truth, positivism, love). I would not have believed it had I not seen it with my own two eyes, but it appears as though America has just given birth and is the proud parent of a healthy, beautiful bouncing baby boy hurricane. All his vital signs are excellent. He is increasing in speed and power by the second exponentially. Winds of strength and love clocked at 2,500 mps already, and judging by "the pair" on this kid, he is going to have a major impact on this country—for the good, of course. So hold on tight. We all have a cyclone of potential in each of us. The decision is this: if we tend to the Left, we go backwards and implode—to the right, we move forward and explode with positivism.

# BIG GAME HUNTER

People all over the world seem to have a fascination with the thrill of the hunt. Think about it, people hunt for a mate, for food and water, for shelter, for sport, for happiness or treasure, for success, or for their destiny/purpose. There are all kinds of things to hunt for, but the most dangerous of all is the Big Game Hunter. For it is possible for the hunter to become the hunted, if he is not careful, which leads me to my point. There is one other type of game that is very elusive, very dangerous, and extremely hard to track because of where it dwells and how it moves. You'd never know it was there until after the fact. The animal that I am referring to is a humongous elephant that takes up to half of America. This spiritual pachyderm has been the cause of so much death and destruction that it cannot be calculated.

I am sure you have all heard the saying, there's an elephant in the room, yet no one seems to be able to get a good look at it. Since this rogue calf is a spiritual beast, she dwells in the hearts and minds of people who yield themselves to be used by her. The truly sad part about it is that people see the effects of it and they know where it is, yet because of political correctness, certain people can't say a word. If they did, they could have their homes, lives and careers trampled and torn to pieces with one slip of the tongue. So don't doubt the reality of this killer.

This is why a spiritual Big Game Hunter comes in handy. Because he can say things and go where others cannot. A B.G.H. has to have the speed, wisdom, and strength to track and subdue his quarry.

# THE OFFER

After much thought and consideration, I have decided to come out of retirement and track and/or capture or kill this rogue so that America may be saved. This is why I am making an offer to the conservative right "Reps," that if each conservative will donate only one little dollar, it should give me enough capital to build a state of the art command and control center to hunt this calf. Even though this is an allegory, it is a very serious condition—not to be taken lightly.

This may come as a shock to some of you, but the vast majority of the crimes of passion, as well as violent crimes, are committed by people with an emotionally based ideology. "Do what you feel and if it feels good, do it."

I don't know about you, but I am so tired of seeing little children or innocent men and women being molested or killed and raped all because some people are so out of control they can't keep perverted, violent emotions under control. The best way to stop the body is to sever the head. I think this would be a way to kill four birds with one stone. 1) We can show solidarity; 2) we need a head count; 3) we may be able to save this country; and 4) can you think of a better way to drive the "Left" absolutely insane. Albeit as short a drive as it would be, this would really stick in their craw—a Black man who leaves their plantation only to rise up on the Right and lead the charge that would lead to their demise. How cool would that be?

Because of the vicious attack she is putting on the White House, we are going to need all the help we can get in '08, so think it over. America is waiting. The best way to stop this attack which is splitting and destroying this country from the inside-out is to cut off the spiritual food supply, which are people who are weak-minded, either because they have been lied to or they do not have a sense of self-worth or esteem. A combination of the two will always cause a person to become a victim. "The truth cuts like a knife, hurts like hell, yet heals like Heaven." The best way to launch a counter-attack is to inject massive amounts of truth into the body of the beast that will thereby educate the food source to the truth, which will have a tranquilizing effect.

Once the pachyderm is sedated, we can load her into a cage with a frame made of morality, and bars made of respect, responsibility, and discipline. Then she can be loaded along with all her handlers in the Liberal, Socialist Democratic party onto a ship, then sent overseas to the Frenchy French, where they can live on a wild life preserve for the rest of their days, driving poor weak-minded people to the brink of insanity with their self-pity, dependent, victim, disenfranchised mentality.

# WEAKMINDEDNESS

What came first, the chicken or the egg? In other words, is a person addicted to crack cocaine before or after he was addicted to weakness? What about sexaholics and alcoholics, etc?

The only other thing I would like to say on the topic is my definition of being weak-minded. I define it as any thing or person, or ideology, or movement (political, cultural, social), that will cause a person to turn against God Himself or his or her fellow man.

I know a lot of people will be offended by the term "weak-minded," yet the truth of the matter is we all have strengths and weaknesses. There are also two forces that pull against each other in the form of good versus evil. This split is personified in our emotions versus our intellect. In other words, doing what we feel as opposed to doing what we know is right. For example, smoking cigarettes or weed (marijuana) can bring you a certain amount of pleasure, yet if you stop to think about the possible damage to your health, physically and mentally, would you still do them? If so, you are weak.

What about sexually giving yourself to people you are not married to or made to be with sexually? Obviously it feels good, yet do you really stop to think about what this says about your self-respect, self-worth and self-esteem? What in the world is worth gaining and losing touch with your own soul? What about listening to music that fills your heart and mind with lust, violence, anger, hate, laziness, and glorifies drug addiction and criminal behavior? The music may sound good and make you feel good, but have you stopped to think what kind of effect it will have on your true quality of life? (By the way, all the characteristics of this type of music are based in weak-mindedness and fear.)

What about the Liberal Democrats' promotion of entitlement programs. Yes, it feels good for people to give you "free" money and a home, but what affect does that have on your freedom, independence, dignity, and future; your motivation, your goals, hopes, and dreams? Is a few dollars worth all of that? Most people become angry, jealous, ungrateful and bitter because they have trapped themselves in a lifestyle that does not give them room to grow as a human being spiritually, emotionally and intellectually.

This is the extreme danger with emotional, over-sympathetic Liberal Socialist ideology. They make basket cases out of otherwise normal men and women. This is the root cause of all the problems in our culture. If we do not address these issues, things will only get worse and worse. The civil liberties that the Libs claim to support are the ones that will cause you to enslave yourself, thereby making you easy to control and manipulate. This will ultimately lead to your being on a path of self-destruction.

When does a "perp" know that his brainwashing attack was successful? When the "vic" is hell bent on self-destruction, i.e. gangster rappers. Black-on-Black crime is spiritual cannibalism. Less morality equals more depravity. We are our culture, our culture is us.

One might ask why Libs want to undermine the spiritual fiber (morality) of our nation. What is their ultimate goal for this nation? Why do they subvert our culture with weakness? I think it is obvious to see that they have an ulterior motive. If weak is as weak does, then their plans can't mean anything good for America, especially those at the bottom of the barrel.

It would be nice if they would simply admit what their long term goals are for America, and their long term plans to accomplish it. Since political ideologies affect every facet of the American experience from business to culture, to religion, to foreign affairs, a political ideology is the head of all the people who vote for that particular party, Conservative or Liberal.

We as Americans need to have dialogue as to what direction the nation should go—to the Left or the Right. Because we are tearing this nation apart, and if that happens, we will all lose.

# FOR YOUR CONSIDERATION

If life was like a card game of Spades with suits of politics, culture, economy/business, ace Diamonds, ace Hearts, and ace Clubs respectively, then spirituality would be the ace of Spades and would trump everything like the "Don." The reason for this is that all the rest emanate from the spiritual realm.

A reliable way to tell if you are reading or hearing spiritual truth is to see if all the major "hats" of society fit. For instance, in these excerpts are the work of an architect, attorney, teacher, surgeon, police officer, firefighter and soldier to name a few. America is now fighting two wars—one inside the country, the other outside; one spiritual, one physical. Both enemies emanate from the same source, "weakness."

Weakness, unlike strength, does not require any intellect, just emotion or to put it another way, unlike the truth, lies don't require any intelligence, just ignorance. The spiritual war the Libs sought to wage in the dark ignorance of night will now be fought in the spiritual light of intelligence of the day.

The Libs own the culture, movies, music, clothes, television, newspapers, public schools and colleges, so time is on their side. At the rate they are going, eventually they will win by sheer numbers. If the Right does not wake up, stop sitting around playing tiddlywinks, and realize we are not wrestling against flesh and blood, we will all be sitting around those little tables outside a café or bistro with horizontally striped turtlenecks and those funny little hats sipping a latte and eating croissants, while a man plays Frère Jacques on an accordion. While our unemployment rises over ten percent, some people blow up cars and churches, and we sit and ponder why they do such things. So in the words of Ms. Ingram, "Let's roll up our sleeves and go to work."

The thing that the Libs don't quite understand is that in order to be qualified as a "god," you have to meet not only the physical needs as well as the spiritual side of a person or race. One thing you need to remember, the only thing that will keep a Lib from being defensive or going on the attack, is to tell them what they want to hear. Let them win, which is the essence of intolerance, giving birth to "political correctness" which is nothing but "social terrorism." Do what I say or else.

Pacifists on the Left mistakenly view their cowardly unbalanced view of world affairs, (i.e. War in Iraq) as a Godly road to the moral high ground. In actuality, anyone who would let an evil enemy come to his home or land and destroy his family and friends is a sniveling, spineless, cowardly fraud seeking appeasement. As much as you are weak, is as much as your enemy hates you and the weaker you become, the faster he will pursue you. It is sort of like the way the Left pursues the Right.

A tale of two ideologies: Conservatives versus Liberals, intellect versus emotions, Capitalism versus Socialism, independence versus dependence, tolerance versus intolerance, and morality versus immorality.

The greatest thing about becoming a conservative is that by necessity you must become an intellect, which gives you an awesome ability to better use the great power of choice. This implies options to choose from, as in right or wrong or the lesser of two evils. Either way, you are in control of your destiny. As opposed to being emotional, you are under control of how you feel—right or wrong, good or bad. At this point, because of your lack of control, your destiny becomes your fate because of your inability to control yourself. A person in control of his own destiny is a prime candidate to be independent, to make his own way, a Capitalist, positive, strong and free. A person who is emotional is a prime candidate to become dependent—to have someone take care of them like a child, i.e. Socialism. A person who can't control himself is usually weak, negative, and slavish. Another thing about a person who is in control of himself is that he can choose to be tolerant or intolerant because some things in life require tolerance, but other things should not be tolerated. On the other hand, people who are weak, dependent, and emotional cannot afford to see the other side of the coin so they cannot tolerate anything or one who is in opposition to how they "feel" things should be. They are extremely intolerant. Right or wrong, it's all about how they feel, feel, feel, feel!

And last but not least, morality is practically defined as a person who chooses between the high and the low road and chooses the former. The dependent, emotional persons only care about how and what makes them feel good. So, who would you want to live next to, a person who has respect for himself and your property or someone who thinks because of how he feels and thinks he can disrespect your home and family because of the way he feels?

# GOING TO TRIAL

Hear ye! Hear ye!! Hear ye!!!. The first and only one of its kind in American history, the trial of the civilized world is about to commence. All rise! All rise! The Most High and Honorable and Holy and Righteous and Glorious Judge of the universe, the Lord God Almighty presiding. The case that is being brought before the high court is a class action, five count indictment with multiple cases into the millions. The defendant is the Liberal Socialist Democratic party. The plaintiffs are: 1) God, 2) America, and 3) Black Americans. Since this is a spiritual trial, the case will be tried in the hearts and minds of the American people.

I need as many Americans as possible to hear (330 million) this indictment. We can then decide the truth and what is best for the nation, that we may keep from destroying her or tearing her apart, because a house or nation divided against itself cannot stand.

The first count is on behalf of God Almighty. For in my observation, the Liberal regressive party is doing everything in its awesome power to remove the knowledge of God from this country, even though the founding fathers made it very well known that He (God) would always be welcome in America. Yet every time I turn on the news or pick up a paper, one of your cohort atheists, A.C.L.U., etc. are trying to get prayer out of school or God out of the pledge of allegiance to the U.S. flag, or nativity scenes taken down, or the term "Merry Christmas" eradicated, or the Ten Commandments removed from court houses, or crosses removed from state seals, or God's name removed from our currency of all things. I can see why you want a separation between church and state—because you fear Him.

Nevertheless, part two of the first charge is most grievous and heinous. For one of the Ten Commandments states that anyone that has a relationship with God shall have no other God before Him. Yet, in my opinion, your party has set yourself up to be as a god to the Black race, in that they look to you instead of God to meet their needs. If I may be so bold as to speculate on the mind of God, this sounds like idolatry, as you seek to replace Him as sovereign Lord (by the way, I might add that you have failed miserably since the vast majority of our youth are hell bent on self destruction).

This leads me to the second count, even though on the surface you pretended to be our friends with all of your "free money" programs, when in actuality you used this to handicap and enslave my race with brainwashing to the degree that 90% of them will not leave the plantation. They are wasting their lives never knowing or realizing all the love and potential God has for them and has placed in them. You are grievously complicit because you actually blame the Republicans for being the cause of our plight, when it was you all along. By the way, I will be taking the White guys' case pro-bono; because of the large elephant in the room, they can't even defend themselves without being labeled a racist, bigot, etc.

Anyway, back to the second count from the Black religious perspective, you have incited them to commit idolatry because they look to man instead of God—90% of them anyway. And since you have lied as to the culprit, you have filled their hearts with bitterness, unforgiveness, anger and jealousy, mad about what someone else has. This has brought about a spirit of ingratitude with God because with all of the blessings and benefits in this greatest nation in the history of the world, they are still unhappy and angry.

The third charge is because of the different factions of the Liberal baby killers who hate life, men who like being women, women who like being men, women who hate the God-ordered patriarchy, and people who want God out of His own land, which all amounts to the world's point of view. They are spiritually in bed with all of these people, which amounts to spiritual adultery by the casting of their vote for your party. How can they claim to build God's kingdom by voting for the people that are trying to tear it down? Can a house divided stand?

The fourth count in this charge is concerning my race, the secular portion, which is being devastated by the house Negroes, Aunt Jemimas, and Uncle Toms that you have helped to set up to oppress and play on my people's hurt and wounded feelings, as if we have not been through enough in this country. We need time to heal the wounds of slavery that have pierced our very souls. The Father has cattle on a thousand hills for us to claim in His name. Your house Negroes try to keep us upset over 40 acres and a mule, some so-called reparations. To you, we are nothing but crops. All you want from us is our money and our votes. You only give us token jobs in your empire. Your contempt for us has reached Heaven and His answer is coming. You have engineered pain and misery in my people, so many broken homes, deaths and people in jail. With tears in my eyes, I lay the charge of spiritual rape against your party. With your lies of being a disenfranchised victim, we are being left behind and have now created our own sub-culture in which Black-on-Black crime is rampant. This is nothing but "spiritual cannibalism." We are devouring each other's lives and potential, over money, cars, jewels, sex, clothes and fame. You may wish to call me radical or extreme, but this side is temporary. What's on the other side is <u>forever.</u> So are those things worth taking that chance?

The fifth indictment is on behalf of America herself. Based on the cultural/spiritual revolution that the Liberals launched in the '60s, the vast majority of the subsequent fallout of social problems was started in the family or the lack thereof, as well as the criminal justice system to the callous, indifferent, apathetic attitude of society. You can't tell what's trustworthy because everyone is looking out for what makes them feel good. This is akin to spiritual sedition and the high crime of spiritual treason to undermine the moral fabric of this nation. For a nation's ability to stand in adversity depends on the strength of the hearts and minds of its people to stand together for the good of all. Yet you continue to promote divisive and subversive attitudes that keep this nation weak and off-balance.

You even have the audacity to use the war in Iraq for political purposes just to try and bring down the President, all the while not caring about our troops on the ground in harm's way. This is absolutely giving aid and comfort to the enemy. The enemy knows if they will kill one more of our troops, they hope that it will be enough to force the President to turn and retreat which would be a disaster for Iraq, as well as the U.S.A. Talk about a lose-lose situation.

Then there are the slanderous attacks that you have made against the "Right," which I remember and have been searching for proof of for years, however, I have not found conclusive evidence that they are secretly holding my race back. The only people I see doing that are the Democrats. That is why I am taking their case pro bono, as stated before, so we can get to the bottom of the matter. For this has been the cause of much division in America. Therefore, please provide all your evidence ASAP. I was told that this is the land of opportunity, not a hand-out. An American has the freedom and right to work and learn all they want to, to support and raise their family to the best of their ability. Even though this is the most benevolent and generous nation in the history of the world, there is no law that says in a free society a person has to help you, if they don't have a mind to do so. Yet in America, for people who don't walk around with a chip on their shoulders or feelings on their sleeves, this is rarely the case. There is always someone willing to help people who want to better themselves. You may have to look about, but they are out there—trust me because I'm one of them.

Well, I could go on and on, but I think you get the gist of the charges. I await your response so we might resolve these issues in an expeditious and timely manner. Your cooperation is greatly appreciated.

The Spiritual Attorney

# FINAL NOTES - CLOSING ARGUMENTS

1. Our zeal for each other sets us against each other's enemies. Who knew they would both be in the Liberal Democratic Party.

2. The purpose and reason for spirits is to reach and maximize their full potential in your life. Weak belong to weak and strong belong to strong. Hate wants to be as weak as you can be made to feel. Love wants to be strong as you can be made to believe. As is love, joy, kindness, patience, goodness, forgiveness versus hate, lust, anger, unforgiveness, jealousy, etc.

3. Independents in the political realm, I hate to tell you, don't exist. In the spiritual realm, there are only two sides of the coin. So Doc Savage, please bring your nation into the fray wholeheartedly, that you may rest at night.

4. This is not about the color of the skin, black or white, but a color of the heart, black or white. We must save America.

5. Is it any wonder why the Left wants to separate church and state to keep Americans apart from God, that they may take control of our lives and have us "worship man?" You decide for yourself, but for me and mine, we will follow the voice of the Lord, render to Caesar what is Caesar's, and to God what is God's.

6. Light and dark, strength and weakness, good and evil, can't actually occupy the same space at the same time. When a Liberal tries to convince you to be tolerant of their feelings and their views, and since they are super-hyper-ultra-mega sensitive, when they say, "Be considerate," that means anything you say will upset them and hurt their feelings, which is essentially social terrorism. They are telling you to hold still until they grow big enough or find a big enough stick to knock your block off.

7. People talk about not being so judgmental, when in

actuality a person judges themselves based on the "truth" or the "lie," "strength" or "weakness," "right" or "wrong." Just because a person knows the difference between the two does not make them judgmental, just observant.

8.  The only thing harder to learn to do than like yourself is to love yourself.

9.  The political and religious leaders of the Black Americans in this country are not actually leaders, but more like followers. They are being led by the Liberal Democratic Party, which is the party of "angry white women." They are leading you with "milk" and an apron string. The thing you must understand about the spiritual realm is that that which is done on the surface is superficial, and the only way you know whether an act was a facade is that the end result is the direct opposite of the stated intent. The "Libs" would have you think that they have your best interest at heart via welfare and entitlement programs, which is the complete opposite of what they really desire for us. They really seek to pacify and then re-enslave us again. I hope you don't think they have a problem with giving you "other people's money" just to distract you and lull you into a false sense of security. The "angry white woman's" real agenda is to turn God's ordained patriarchal order into an ungodly matriarchal disorder. The same feminine spirit is at work in France and Germany with their 10% and 11% unemployment, and their 1.3% economic growth, while the U.S. is at 5% and 3.5% respectively. Can you imagine how bad this would be for Black Americans since our unemployment is actually more like 10% in the 'hood. It would be a disaster for us to let these "angry white women" continue to lead our race. The Black "political and religious followers" in this country have led 90% of our race into the valley of the shadow of death. The Black Americans that are 40 years old and older had a chance to take advantage of the manufacturing and industrial revolution before it faded. Therefore, we have retirement plans, 401(k)'s, homes, savings and security more so than

the younger generation. America has switched to the hi-tech revolution and our youth are being left behind because of the followers in politics and the church who apparently like following an angry white woman around. And if that is not bad enough, we have a gang of Uncle Tom/gangster rappers telling our youth that the only things worth living for are drugs, sex, money, crime, and violence. This is as the valley of death (follow the money, Libs, own the movie, music, clothing, alcohol, and tobacco industries. Who is pimping who?) Emotionally they are made bitter, hurt, and full of self-pity. Intellectually I have heard more than a few Black kids say that trying to be an intelligent Black kid is "acting White." A lot of them just go to school to meet someone to make a baby they can't take care of. Spiritually they don't have a clue as to all the potential and gifts God placed in them and His strong desire to be with them everyday of their lives, through the good and bad. Physically we know Black-on-Black crime is off the hook, the page, and off the chain. They are trapped and are stacking up on each other. Since they are the future of our race, I think we need to go in and help them find a way out of this meat grinder, and please don't tell me about other races. Ours was specifically targeted for destruction, and those other races are just copy-cats, because Black "rappers" have made being dirty and filthy look good. The flames of their fire will burn any weak-minded person available. The reason people can't see this slavery is because you can't see the forest for the trees. You have to take a step back and let your mind clear from the weakness of believing that this is the way things are meant or supposed to be. If you political and religious leaders have the courage to stand up in 2008, and let that angry white woman know we are no copies, slaves, then maybe our kids would start to listen to us again and want to make something out of their lives to carry on our history and struggle to be free at last, free at last, Praise God Almighty, free at last.

10. M.L.K.'d –this is what happens to a Black man who truly

stands up for God, his country, and his race. The only good thing about that would be the "martyr effect."

11. It is not that God is in a box, but He has pretty much been locked out of the sub-culture on the Left.

12. In order to make it fair, God has set Himself at a complete and total disadvantage that makes you have to look really hard to find and understand Him in the course of your life.

13. When you see the sea of sin, He saved your soul from, surely salvation will satisfy your soul and life will begin to be sweet again.

14. Blacks, Whites and Hispanics that are trapped in the sub-culture: things will never get better for us until we put a stop to the source of the weakness—the Libs in D.C.

15. I believe the Hispanic people have good hearts and great honor, once they've seen the truth. And I also believe that once Blacks are detoxified of weakness, they too will choose to leave the "spiritual plantation."

16. The Libs in D.C. and their radical social insurgents are the last people to talk about an atmosphere or culture of corruption. They themselves are the instigators of a spiritual culture of corruption that has brought America to her knees.

17. In order to make the Bible come "alive," preachers and pastors must do as the Lord did in His day, deal with the evil where it thrives. This is what will cause revival and cause the Body of Christ to stand up, unite, mobilize, and stop all their petty bickering amongst themselves. Speaking in tongues, clothes to wear, places to go or not go, food to eat or not, etc.

18. The Libs in Washington and the media always accuse the conservatives on the Right; that they are nothing but "angry white men." It only stands to reason that they on the "Left" must be the opposite, thus "angry white women." What are

they angry about, you ask? They are angry about a male-run society. They believe it is the cause for all the trouble in the country and the world. So they have embarked on a campaign, which is a combination of projecting all of their weakness and immorality on America and the Right, also with the pacification and neutralization of the Black race and the subsequent sub-culture, and last but not least the appeasement of Radical Islamic Muslims (R.I.M.). All three of their strategies are based in lies, deception and weakness. Their plans will ultimately back-fire and all who support them will help bring major damage to America and the world. If God would have them be in charge, He would have made it so. I am personally not mad at women overall, I like and love them. But right is right, and wrong is wrong. We cannot afford to give control of this nation over to people who can't see past their own selfish desires and ambitions.

19. Isn't it refreshingly ironic that in this country the God of the Bible not only gives you a choice to believe or not, but also if you choose Him, He says, stand still and see the salvation of the Lord (Exodus 14:13, also 2 Chronicles 20:17). He will fight the battle because He will defend His word. All He wants us to do is tell the truth and stand on it as opposed to other "faiths" that require their members to blow themselves and others up as a sign of devotion. After all, the battle for humanity is being waged in the hearts and minds of individuals, so why blow them up? Why not let people decide for themselves. The battle is the Lord's.

20. There are only two spiritual fires that live (burn) in the hearts and minds of men. The fire of the truth and the fire of the lie. The two are diametrically opposed to each other eternally. The one is actually warm, living and loving; the other is cold, dying and hateful. To deny the truth as real automatically sets you against it. Have you ever been camping or to a barbecue? When you start a fire, you need three components; the ignition (match), fuel (wood, coal), and oxygen (life). The same is true for spiritual fire; the

135

spark is truth, the fuel is love, and the oxygen is the unlimited potential of your life.

For the record, in the entire history of the world there is or has only been one being who claimed to have come down from Heaven, and claimed to be the Son of God. He also identified, confronted and defeated mankind's silent ominous enemy, Satan. This is the truth; whether you believe it or not, you cannot change it. I tried for 20 years to find a loophole—there is none. The Lord and Savior Jesus Christ died for the sins (weaknesses) of the world. This is the love that God has towards us, that we should live a life full of strength, love, joy, and peace. This is the kingdom of light and truth, and everything else is the kingdom of darkness and lies. I hate to sound mean or to hurt anyone else's feelings about their religion, or sound arrogant or intolerant, but you cannot appease or tolerate darkness because it will swallow you up and you may not even know it.

Other religions try, by the performance of a set of rituals, to give man the external appearance of holiness, yet the heart and mind is where the battle takes place. That's where God goes to work—on the inside, not outside. The only other thing I can say is that people who believe and accept God's plan is that we have both fires burning in our lives, the old one and the new one (born again). That is why Believers still do things from the old ways because the two are at war in our lives. And in the world, some people are quick to call a child of God a hypocrite when they see them doing wrong. But at least they have the courage to try and do what's right. Depending upon what a person has been through in life, their sanctification can take a pretty long time to accomplish. I hope this explanation helps some people cut through all the lies of darkness that are being spread around the world and country. The thing about deception and lies is that they can take many different forms such as a government or cultural movement as a type of "God" or science or nature, not to mention an individual. With all these factions out here it is no wonder why people are so confused and disheartened. People are looking for the door, but it is difficult to be sure with so many distractions and temptations. "So little time, so many lies!"

## JUST MORE STUFF

The truth has the power to split you in two (spiritually speaking). The left is weak, emotionally unstable and dependent. The right is strong, intellectual and independent. It is a combination of your personality, environment (culture), up-bringing and wisdom, or the lack thereof, that will determine which side you will lean towards and how far you will either fall or grow.

Give a man a fish, you feed him for a day; teach him how to fish, you feed him for a life time.

Libs can tolerate any and everything, except the truth.

If a doctor told you that you had a deadly form of cancer, would you want to kill it or tolerate it? Well, Liberalism and Socialism are spiritual and cultural cancers to yourself and America. What do you opt to do? Even if you don't believe in God and the truth, do what's "Right" for yourself and your country. There is a big difference between loving God and being loved by God. One is a two-way street; the other is a one way.

*The best way to stay broke is to keep crying broke (your confession will be your possession).*

What do a house of cards and a house of lies have in common? A strong wind can topple them both.

There is only one way to make America whole, and it has two options, either we move to the left or we move to the right. The question is which direction is better for us all— to move forward in time or backward in time? Since the past is dead, let the dead live in the past. The future holds promise, so let those who have life look to the future.

# MESSAGE TO THE TROOPS

I and all those who truly love America greet you and salute you for your courage, commitment and sacrifice. There are scarcely words to express my gratitude, pride and respect for the mission in Iraq and Afghanistan in which you are now engaged.

For now I am convinced that if we had not taken the war to those who hate America, then we would be fighting the war over here. The memory of 9/11 will never be forgotten. May all those who are complicit be brought to justice, both foreign and domestic. It is with shock and dismay that I am compelled to witness the extremely dangerous and perilous times in which we now live.

It has become apparent and obvious to me that America is fighting two wars, on two fronts, and in two realms—one physical, one spiritual. For while you are over there fighting, dodging bullets and bombs, trying to stay alive and to complete the mission, the exact same can be said of the war front over here in the U.S. The same men and women, bullets and bombs, are going off over here, except they are spiritual in that they are launched from the hearts and minds of those who hate America.

I know hate is a strong word, yet to speak out in such a negative manner while there are boots on the ground, is tantamount to giving aid and comfort to our enemies. This behavior I find to be traitorous, inexcusable, and intolerable. They may well have cost American lives by encouraging our enemies to keep fighting in hopes that we would cut and run, which would only embolden our enemy, and make the world and the U.S. less safe. It is for this reason and a few others that I have decided, as you are fighting and risking your lives over there against a physical adversary, that I am compelled to do the same over here against our spiritual one. Even though I have concluded that they both emanate from the same source, "weakness."

As of 12/04/05, I am an army of one and I will do everything in my power, hopefully with the help of my fellow "real" Americans, to lay down suppressing fire and draw their attention off you and the

President. By all means, may you may complete the mission and return home as the heroes you are. In all honesty, I have not always been so patriotic. In fact, it was the last Presidential election in 2004 that my eyes were opened to the truth. Thanks to the spiritual Underground Railroad, I was able to escape the repressive, abusive, cruel and heartless Liberal Democratic plantations and P.O.W. camps of the proverbial South. I was able to make my way up north to be a free man. You heard me right, the Lib Dems have succeeded in re-enslaving 90% of Black Americans through hand-outs, lies and psy-ops (i.e. military term for psychological operations). We have been spiritually, emotionally and mentally whipped into believing that we can't make it on our own, that we need help all the time. They have convinced us that we are disenfranchised victims who are not actually part of America, so be safe and stay on a plantation and let the government take care of you.

I have been whipped and beaten with these lies for over 40 years. I am tired and wounded spiritually, and I need a few years to rest, yet my race and country need me. I am reminded of John F. Kennedy who stated, "Ask not what your country can do for you— ask what you can do for your country."

The thing that needs to be understood about living on a plantation, is that the vast majority of residents think it is America's fault, so they don't care what happens to the country. They may actually hope something bad happens to shake things up, in which case they could escape from their prison (like down in New Orleans). They can't see who it is who has enslaved them, so they blame Republicans because Libs point the finger of blame and say, "sic 'em." That's why when Blacks leave the plantation they are attacked, ridiculed, mocked and put to shame for being patriotic and loving this great nation. They don't realize, due to ingratitude and thinking that life or somebody owes them something versus what they owe themselves, and are not thinking that they have it much better than our ancestors—who had real chains around their necks—or our distant relatives still in Africa who are suffering, starving to death, and/or being murdered by evil men. They have so much to be thankful for, but as long as they stay on the plantation, they will never know what it feels like to have a country to call home. If not here, then where?

Since the Black race has been beaten and brainwashed for over 80 years, it is no wonder why Black-on-Black crime is the way it is. With every passing generation we are on the slow road to self-destruction, which is a form of insanity. This is not only my race, but America as well that will cease to exist as per her constitution, if we do not put a stop to these Libs. As I said, these are perilous and grave times in which we live, never mind what's on the surface, those are just distractions. It is the heart and soul of this nation that is dying, which is the last beacon of truth, liberty and life in the world. It is time for all people with the spirit of freedom in their hearts, black, white, brown, yellow, and red to stand together for the good of our country and our home. America!!!

Now having said all of the above, to the soldiers over there, you may rest well assured that there are spiritual boots on the ground in the U.S.A. They are big and black like yours, but they are not made for just walking and marching. Since I am prior military, go Navy! I think the best way to frame this spiritual, cultural and political battle for America is the context of the, I dare say, greatest sea battle of all times.

The mission: Save America. The target: the USS Queen Dem Lib Immoral (Q.D.L.) Feminist, and her vast armada and supply and fuel network (i.e. newspapers, Lib judges, T.V. news networks, Hollywood, a large part of the music industry, A.C.L.U., most unions, Lib college professors, all public schools, and last but not least their "Black Gold." (the people of the spiritual plantations, the social P.O.W. camps, and the sub-culture.) This I think is the key to victory for America.

Because of her hatred for the President, for defeating both of her two sons (Gore and Kerry), the USS Q.D.L. has come out with all guns blazing trying every trick in the book to bring down our President, which has caused her to attack our troops and Christians. She will do anything to get her power back. "Hell hath no fury like a woman scorned." Yet in her blind rage, she has inadvertently over-extended herself for now she is surrounded on three sides: 1) North: the President is kicking butt so far with the economy and national security, 2) West: the troops in Iraq and Afghanistan are winning the war on terror, 3) East: Christians are holding the heartland at bay. This is where the plot thickens, since she has revealed her positions and strengths, and we know where her supply lines are. All we need is someone from the south to close the door and cut off her supply lines. We could have her surrounded on all four sides, north, south, east and west, and with her supply lines in the rear (south) interrupted or altogether severed, eventually she would go dead in the water. After that we could board her, take the ones who hate America and make them walk the plank—okay, we'll just vote them out of office, so they can fade into obscurity. But not before we all point fingers and laugh at them (they hate that). That's the least they deserve for all the chaos and havoc they have caused.

I figured since I am already behind enemy lines, so to speak, I am in a perfect position to launch a surprise attack from the rear. The "Queen" is arrogant, condescending and has taken my race for granted. She would never suspect that we would turn against her because of all the milk (money) and apron strings (chains), she has led us with. She thinks we are either too dumb, or we have given up, or we are too confused to know who our real enemy is, or just too tired to care. She thinks that the younger generations are just a pack of drug-crazed, sex-crazed, gun-packing gangsta's and hoochies, who are more interested in bottles of bub in the club and shaking tail feathers than preparing their kids to meet the challenges of the future with confidence and optimism. So, like I said, the Queen's hindquarters are naked and fully exposed to me. And fella's, trust me, it ain't a pretty sight. I don't know how much of this I can take before I go blind, God forbid. The things a man will do for God and country and pancakes—there ought to be a law.

I have been hearing some rumors around S.C.C.C. (Spiritual Christian Command Center) that they are about to commission and christen a new class of S.B.S. (Spiritual Battle Ship). I think the name is the USS I AM B. Nemesis. She is as long as seven football fields end to end, and as wide as three fields. Loaded from stem to stern, port to starboard with S.B.T. (Spiritual Bunker-busting Technology), 10", 20", 30", 40" guns and a hull of solid, fortified, impenetrable truth. The S.B.T. is loaded with enough truth to dig down through all the lies, pride, self-pity, anger, unforgiveness, lust, envy, and ingratitude. It will detonate a burst of love and understanding enough to turn a person's life from left to right, from dark to light, from weak to strong, from slave to free, from cold to warm, and from dying to living. If I were the commander of the Nemesis, I would move at full speed to optimum striking distance, and then cut a path across Q.D.L.'s supply and fuel lines from east to west, back and forth, back and forth—all the while firing port and starboard at 100% fire power with a few million rounds a month landing in the heart of the blue states. Eventually the Queen Lib would have to surrender or be politically, culturally, and spiritually destroyed. Resistance is futile!

After that we could let the real Democrats, who really care about America, have their party back by 2008, i.e. the Joe Lieberman's and Zell Miller's, then we could have a 4$^{th}$ of July as a wholehearted America; one like the universe has never seen. We would be well on the road to completing Dr. Martin Luther King, Jr's dream.

And for the troops "over there," we will keep the music playing, can you hear it? We will keep a light on for you—close your eyes, can you see it? We will keep the grill lit as well, can you smell the aroma? And we will keep a cold one in the chamber for you. God speed.

# MESSAGE TO THE YOUTH

I've heard it said that life is wasted on the youth, even though I don't necessarily agree with that statement wholeheartedly. I guess what the person who made that statement was trying to say is that young people can spend so much of their time (life) going in the wrong direction as far as the things they "value" in life. By the time they realize what's worth truly living for, a good portion (if not all of their lives) are already over with. This "situation" has reached epidemic proportions in this country—kids not having any value or sense of worth with the most priceless gift they have: their very lives.

Even though every person is ultimately responsible for their own actions, I believe that as adults we are largely to blame. Based upon the condition of our youth today (9/23/07 is the date of writing this chapter), we did not set a good example of how to live a strong, free, and independent life. Actually, it was quite the contrary and we have passed that onto our youth to the point where most of the younger generations believe life is all about being cool, tough, and sexy, when in fact they are on the wrong road, leading to a weak, dependent, and worthless life.

We as adults have taken our eyes off of the prize—our youth (you) are that prize, because you are the future. As adults, what joy can we have in life if our kids will not enjoy the gift of life? So, having said all of that, on behalf of all the parents who have abused, abandoned, neglected, or otherwise been indifferent to the well-being of their (or any other) child, I offer my most deep, heartfelt, and sincere apology. I ask for your forgiveness for all of our selfish, backwards, and weak leadership.

Speaking as an African-American, our race seems to be suffering the brunt of this nightmare. The one thing I would like to say to our youth is that after all we have been through in this country, we have come too far to turn back now. As a nation, as a whole, the same applies to other nationalities. Even though I don't actually have any kids, as soon as I find some more like-minded adults to form a coalition of the faithful, we will be coming to you with truth and love to get you turned around in the "right" direction., so that you won't wreck your life in your youth.

Remember, if you are feeling the negative effects of the spiritual darkness that's in you and all around you, just know this…there's a light at the end of the tunnel! His name is Jesus, so keep holding on because we're going to try and get a little hope to you.

P.S. Since according to the truth, the youth are the future of this nation, in my estimation that makes you #1 in my book literally.

God Bless and Keep Holding on,

Amen

# MESSAGE TO THE SENIORS

An apology is owed to all of America's African-American Senior Citizens. I cannot overlook extending my personal and sincere apology to millions of our wonderful seniors who have collectively done so much to help raise our youth up to this point in our American history. Whatever you do, despite the fact that some mindless individuals (like one of Colorado's former, Liberal Democratic Governors who called all seniors "useless eaters"– how's that for being the party of the average working classes) have tried to marginalize your value as cherished and contributing members of today's totally selfish society. They are just another part of the "me" generation, so don't ever let anyone make you feel like you cannot contribute anything of value anymore, to anyone; that's absolute nonsense!

As individuals, and also as a group, you still have so much to offer all of us, especially for the immediate benefit of our youth. They desperately need your mature advice, which is based on real-life experience and more importantly filled with Godly wisdom.

The tragic absence of "fathers" from the home also creates a huge void that you can help to fill as helpmates to the single moms out there.

We need each one of you to offer your help all across our entire nation and you especially need to share it with America's troubled Black youths. You can help to counteract much of what they are getting in the way of wrong, hate-filled advice from hip-hop role models on MTV and in sitcoms, liberal TV programs, Hollywood's insane flood of blood & guts, video games, DVD's and movies—all combining forces to help our young ones down the wrong paths. If you keep seeing them play in Satan's playground, it shouldn't surprise any of you that way too many of our youth are on an express train to death & hell!

None of those worldly opinion builders would ever think of offering them your kind of Godly advice and wisdom based upon years of Godly living! Just stop and think how critical a role model your parents played in your own lives and that should be more than enough to convince you just how important and valuable you are to our youth. A friendly and loving conversation provided to them at just the right time could easily be a major turning point in their impressionable young lives. That short little talk just might help them stay alive long enough to realize some of their dreams, instead of dying prematurely because of an unwise choice they made to hang with the wrong crowd or worse yet, a street gang.

God's word in the scriptures says, "If you have the ability to do something to be of help to someone in urgent need and you fail to do anything, than it's counted unto you as a SIN OF OMMISSION." That statement alone should make you feel how critically important you are in God's mind, when it comes to reaching out to our youth and offering some Godly choices as an alternative to a path that could lead to premature death.
Remember: Most of the people who fill our cemeteries (including far too many of our youth) died with their dreams still unfulfilled.

# THE CIRCUS

Hurry! Hurry! Hurry! Step right up and get your tickets here!

{Sound of carnival music in the background}

Come one, come all! See the spectacle of a life time for the cost of just one buck; only 100 pennies! See the great and terrible, the one, the only "Queen Kong," better known as Queen Lib, captured in the heartland of America by some brave and free Americans!

{Sound of vendors selling popcorn, peanuts}

Here!! For the cost of a buck, see the Queen that has caused America so much pain and heartache behind spiritual bars of morality, and chains of truth and love.

<Queen Lib fiercely growling and shaking bars of cage>

Think about it folks, because of her there are 40 plus million Americans that will never have set foot on their home soil; little boys and girls that will never have a favorite toy or doll, never run and play like we did, never have a favorite color, outfit, best friend or favorite dish, nor go to school and learn to tie their shoes, read, write, tell time, play sports or hear music, nor learn to drive, go to school, go to church, fall in love, or have their first kiss, nor to dance, to hear someone say, "I love you," to take the first airplane ride, to get a job and get the first paycheck, nor to have a family of their own, so they can have kids of their own to love and cherish. They never got the chance that we had, my fellow Americans. Because of her spiritual enslavement of a race of people who already fought long and hard to survive, only to be tricked into giving up their eternal freedom for material goods, we now know the answer to "what does it profit a man to gain the whole world and lose his soul?" You got it, nothing!

How about our kids, who through TV, music, movies, and the school system (up to and through college), are being taught to be soft, weak, emotional, with low self esteem, and so much so that they spend all their time trying to be accepted, popular and sexy, instead of being the best they can be so they can go as far as they can in America, which is the best place in the world to get an education in the first place. They are systematically being reduced to rebellious basket cases. All of these tragedies are only but a few of the sad effects of Liberalism which, in effect, says it's okay to be your worst if that's the way you "feel," despite whether it harms you, your family or society at large. So hurry, hurry, hurry, step right up, we have a special for a limited time only. One buck, one spank for all the trouble the Queen has caused; ten bucks, ten spanks (for adults only). It is rewarding and therapeutic (if the Excellence in Broadcasting Network, the war room, great Americans, or savage nation would be so kind as to set up a "Save America fund," I can put my war ship to the deep blue sea).

The Commander

# ALL THE PRESIDENT'S MEN

I am proud to be one of all the president's men. He is the first Republican President I voted for since I left the "plantation"—probably the first in my family, since Lincoln freed the slaves, when all Blacks voted Republican. I think it is time for all Blacks to get back to our political "roots." You feel me?

I must admit I was worried about the President as to why he did not defend himself when the Lib Dems attacked. It seemed as though he was afraid of the Libs—I could not figure it out. Then it hit me, the President has so much class and charisma that most of their attacks he would not even dignify with a response. Talk about cool under pressure, he's taking all these attacks while prosecuting a war on terror and keeping the economy booming, which grew 4.3% in November 2005, starting to fix the broader situation. I think I would rate this President with all he's had to go through, as in the top five Presidents in American history. I would say he is a President's President. I think he has earned the right to lead this nation.

Okay, here we go again from a spiritual perspective, the President reminds me of a James Bond figure {James Bond's theme song playing}. Bush 00-43, George W. Bush, he is in a dance of death, a very passionate tango with an angry female for the control and destiny of this nation {tango music playing}. He has a rose clenched in his teeth. She has a dagger in her teeth, not to mention poisonous lipstick. In her purse is a vile of arsenic, a Derringer, and choke wire for a bracelet, all of which she has tried to use on him repeatedly, and yet he is still untouched for the most part. I would almost have to call him the "Teflon President." The President is like a matador who has to fight the biggest bunch of bulls in history, and he's in costume dodging the bull at every turn; tormenting the poor, dumb bull. Olé! The bull tried to "Gore" him in 2000, only to get stuck in the dirt, olé! Viva El-Presidente!

Another bull tried to "Kerry" him off in a stretcher, only to get tangled in his own tongue and still the President is standing. Ole! Viva El Presidente! Ole!!!

The only thing I can agree with you Liberal Democrats on is that this is actually the wrong time for this war. You are right, it should have been fought during the Clinton administration, but he was busy getting busy. And please, it's offensive to me to call him a Black President. What are you really trying to say about my race? If it is anything bad, it is not like we did not have the Libs' help. If you really want to know how I feel, I think the President and Clinton should be put on Mt. Rushmore, only do the back of Clinton's head to symbolize how he turned his back on America. For all his smooth talk (not), all he gave us is what he got, a snow job. Instead of getting the terrorists in check, he was busy "polishing up his act." In case you Marxists think you are going to get this country without a knock-down, drag-out fight, then you have grossly underestimated our love for God and country. If the gloves are coming off, so be it. If we have to dance, then believe me, the men of America are going to lead black, white, brown, red, and yellow. Get it. Lights on, skirts up, we need to see who is who up in this camp. As a matter of fact, you people on the Left have been rude, nasty, and downright disrespectful to God, my race and this country.

I think as a sign of respect and contrition you ladies ought to take a poll and ask the "right" questions to make the President's approval rating go over 95%, so he and his First Lady can have a good laugh on your behalf. He has earned it. This is an offer you ought not to refuse. There might be a bull's head in the Queen's bed. If I have to pull a Cindy Sheehan, and camp out in front of your 2008 Presidential candidates' home until they come out and sign a document renouncing Socialism and Liberalism as failed institutions and ideologies, I will garner all national and international attention just like dear little Cindy. With what you engineered against my race and New Orleans as a backdrop, how well do you think you will do in 2008 and beyond? Since you like the past so much, your movement may wind up in 1885, you Communist.

## NO GUTS, NO GLORY

In case you missed it, the President and our troops are off limits, unless they do something that is really wrong, intentionally and grievously, which I do not think will be done. Yet they have a nation to protect and defend from an enemy that's about four levels weaker than you are. That's why you people can't see what our situation is. Be that as it may, the more you attack them, the more I am coming for you. And since I am in Bin Laden mode for now, I could be standing right next to you, Lib. I could be your waiter, cashier, teller, bell boy, desk clerk, or butler. The more people that see the truth, the more that will be watching you and listening to every word you say. So I would be careful if I were you (not to harm you), just to vote you out of office, and out of colleges, unions, schools, and movements. Your music, movies, and clothes are all fair game—"follow the money."

# THE SPIRITUAL O.R.

I was all set to do an emergency room operation with America as the patient, but I changed my mind at the last minute. I'll just explain where our nation is in the context of a surgical operation with a patient in critical condition. The first thing you need to understand and accept as a bona fide 100% fact is that America is God's country.

Secondly, America is the best thing since sliced bread. I did not say she was perfect, but she is the greatest nation in the history of the world. There is more freedom and opportunity in this country, chances to make money, be educated, travel, raise a family, worship, play ball, race cars, fly to the moon, build cars, own a home—too many things to mention. The infrastructure of this nation is second to none; our roads, banking, postal, and entertainment; there are more activities and food than you can shake a stick at. A lot of us overindulge to our own demise.

The third thing you need to understand is that without the blood in your veins, you would die. The same thing is true about America from a spiritual standpoint. The reason she has come this far so fast is because of morality. It is her blood, and it is what keeps her taking care of all of us. Morality is basically knowing the difference between right and wrong, and choosing to do what is right.

For the good of yourself and your fellow man, the fourth thing you need to understand is that America is the last and best hope for the rest of the world. Just about all other nations are Communist, Socialist, a monarchy, a dictatorship, or radically religious fellows who all spell enslavement, chaos and misery for the ordinary Joe or Jane. The people in those governments have all the power, money, and fun for themselves and their families and friends. The rest of the people can go eat mud cakes for all they care. We are surrounded by nations who do business with us, but want us to be like they are. No thanks. I would rather be free to make my own destiny with God's help. In order for Socialism to work, Americans must not.

The fifth thing you need to understand is that as morality brings life, immorality brings death to self and society. Immorality means being wicked, depraved, and unrighteous. It is the blood of the spiritually dead.

The sixth thing you need to understand is that in the '60s the Liberal Democrats cut America open with those so-called revolutions, illicit sex, drugs, and politics. And by doing so, they set up a transfusion. So for 40 years they have been draining the life out of America and replacing it with death—spiritual death. This is why people are becoming colder, and more depraved, violent, and angry.

The seventh thing you need to understand is her condition. She is weak, her moral pulse is faint, she's pale, she's dizzy, and she is hallucinating, causing weak people to think they are strong. She could fall into a coma. There are vultures circling over her head. She is in danger of dying. Have you ever seen the movie *Night of the Living Dead*? That is what Americans will be, cold-blooded, murderous, hateful monsters. That's what you can see beginning to happen to people now, and it will get worse if we do not put a stop to the Libs soon; if it is not already too late. The message to Blacks, since crap rolls down hill, is that we are at the bottom of the social ladder as a whole with our youth digging a deeper hole for themselves. When the crap goes down, they will be buried. The lesson was right there in New Orleans. The Libs could care less about you; they only want your vote to stay in power so they can keep killing America.

The eighth thing you need to know is the cure. The cure is the truth. This letter is like 330 million cc's of adrenaline in the heart of America to restart her heart, to pump morality again. This excerpt is like a defibrillator set at 330 million volts, one for each American, give or take a few. How do you give a whole nation mouth to mouth resuscitation? Breathe America, breathe! Breathe America, breathe! Come on girl, wake up girl. A one and a two and a three. I love you America, please wake. Hit her with the defib – clear – clear. Hit – pulse still weak – give me 10 million cc's of truth hooked to an I.V. What's her pressure? Still low, come on, come on honey, you can do it. Please, baby, I just found you, I can't lose you now. Breathe America – beep – beep – she's flat-lining, hit her with the defib – clear – clear. "Hit." Beep, beep, beep, beep. She's stabilizing; her temperature is coming down, get her over to intensive care. It's going to be a long night, but she's in God's hands. I want her under 24/7 supervision. Don't take your eyes off her. If we lose her, what will we give to our kids?

America is dying spiritually. Can you help her? Will you help her? To show that you care for her, all you have to do is care for yourself. The more people that care for themselves, the stronger America will become. When you have been born or raised to be weak (emotional/self-pity), it will be the hardest transition you will ever make day by day.

The Surgeon

# IF THE LEGAL BRIEFS FIT

These are the last, few brief comments on the case of the Lib Dems versus Black race, America, and God.

*News Flash! This Just In!*

If it were not for the fact that I would not want to say anything bad or negative about the Three Stooges out of respect for them, at least they knew they were imbeciles. But what can be said of any good about Kerry, Dean and Martha (Fuller Clark). Why, can someone tell me, do they keep making statements that could embolden our enemies and potentially cost more American lives. Do they know? Do they care or is the pain of being out of power that great that they will say anything to undermine the President and the war effort. God forbid this war will be another Vietnam. Nevertheless, as an act of defense and retaliation on behalf of our troops, every time I hear someone on the Left make a comment or statement, that like Glenn Beck says will make your head explode if it's not wrapped in duct tape. In response to these outlandish remarks from Dizzy Madman Dean's own mouth, I will seek 25,000 votes from your voter base. So 3 x 25,000 = 75,000 votes are owed payable prior to next election. Payment should be made in three equal denominations of Hispanic, White and Black. Thanks for your participation in the voter get back program – Wuub! Wuub! Wuub! Wuub! Wuub! Wuub! Nark! Nark! Nark!

After the last of the legal briefs will be my response to their attacks. Now back to court. Apparently since I am the first person to bring the Lib Dems up on spiritual charges, I guess that would make me the lead attorney. Personally, I was hoping someone else would do it so I could sit back and watch the spectacle of it all. Oh, well, when you get the call from upstairs, you have to take it. I am sure you have heard of my firm, they have been around forever. No really, Father, Son and Holy Ghost L.P.A., B.B.B. I don't mean to sound intimidating, but they have not lost a case ever. That's the reason, like federal prosecutors, I can't prosecute a case unless I am positive of getting a conviction. A conviction in these proceedings is anyone who reads this testimony and changes their heart and mind about your spiritually corrupt party, the more convictions the more your party will cease to exist until you disappear from the political and cultural landscape of America.

I trust that you have been read your spiritual Miranda rights. I know you guys in the A.C.L.U. don't actually believe the Bible is the Word of God, so I guess it won't do any good to tell you where it says "whatever is loosed on earth is loosed in Heaven, and whatever is bound on earth is bound in Heaven." So from a spiritual standpoint, that would make this a legal and binding document whether you believe it or not. You can choose not to believe it, but you may see it again. (Side note to Liberal judges, the Constitution is not a living and breathing document that changes with the extreme radical winds that blow through your empty minds and hearts.) The Constitution is more like a rudder that is solid as a rock, which has guided the good ship America to her place of prominence in the world, and if left alone will continue to guide her to peaceful shores. So please keep your unstable hands and minds off her. If you want a living and breathing document, try this one on for size. These words will live and breathe in the hearts and minds of men and women. Either they will read it, believe it and share it which will cause the fire of truth to grow, or they will not believe it, in which case things will only stay the same. Now, what was the definition of insanity?

In defense of America, there is no such thing as an extremist. To be a guardian of morality, truth, life and love is to be a patriot. We may indeed have to descend to the level of those that would seek to destroy America, whether foreign or domestic. God forbid we should come to the latter.

While I was going over notes for this big case, it occurred to me that in the spiritual realm there are only two sides of the coin, and since everything emanates from the spiritual realm, one side or the other, and since I am a junior partner at Father, Son and Holy Ghost L.P.P., that means that the A.C.L.U. must be representing the "adversary." I hear the Mafia takes notes from him on how to stay low, low, low key. He's so low key he doesn't even want people to know he exists. The reason for that is because people are a lot easier to control when they think they are in control of their own lives. Example: look at how the Libs did Black people in this country. Any way, here's a test if you think you are in control of your life, stop overeating, smoking cigarettes or doing drugs and alcohol, or stop cheating on your wife or husband or sleeping with people you are not married to, or stop gossiping, lying, cheating, stealing or being proud and jealous, or feeling sorry for yourself, etc. These are all weak things that will eventually cause the adversary to steal, kill or destroy the quality of your life, and society and the potential thereof. He is the expressed power and image of weakness. Now, do you see why God had to send His only Son? Because without truth, mankind would be hopeless and helpless. Now do you see why you need a Savior? I admit I am a little curious. How are you A.C.L.U.'ers going to get your client to take the stand? Are you going to subpoena him? Will he be sequestered? Inquiring minds would like to know.

Pop Quiz: Here's a question for the A.C.L.U., the Liberal judges and the Liberal college professors. What do you think is the best course of action? To ignore me and hope I will just go away (which I won't). To ignore me would not give credibility to my case, yet you would remain under attack. You can't afford to actually have your base know the truth about you and who your boss is. Or, do you acknowledge my charges against you, thereby giving credibility to my case against you in the hopes that you might use whatever means at your "pop's" disposal to silence me? If you know the Gospels, then you know that this is basically the Jesus martyr effect. What would have happened had they not tried to stop Him by crucifying Him, which was God's plan all along? So what would you do, ignore me or stop me? What do you do? What do you do? P.S. I will not be ignored!!

When God first gave me His "Laundry List" back when I was 20 years old, I said to Him, "what are you trying to do, get me killed?" That's when I put on my running shoes and ran and ran and ran for 20 years until I could not run anymore. The calling and the election of the Lord are irrevocable, either do it or else. And trust me; you don't want to know what the "or else" is. That, plus the fact that the "Book" says he who seeks to save his life will lose

157

it (in vanity). And he that loses his life for His sake will find it (spreading eternal life). There is no greater call in life than to make a direct contribution to life by helping your fellow man find life.

Anyway, getting back to the list, He wanted me to see if I could shutdown as many spiritual plantations and P.O.W. camps (sub-culture) as possible, and also to remove that tumorous cancer from the Left side of the brain of America, which would cause her to be whole again—one nation under God with liberty and justice for all. Last, but not least, to put a force shield of love and truth around the kids K-12 so they can enjoy their childhood and grow up to be positive, healthy men and women who love their country. Yes, I know it's a dangerous job, but somebody's got to do it—or at least try.

So after He gave me 20 years to travel the world and see the condition of myself and man, good and bad, He told me it was time for my fifteen minutes of fame. I told Him if the pen is mightier than the sword, then He could take fourteen minutes back because this won't take but a minute, once I get in it. What I mean, in case someone thinks I'm being arrogant, is that when you read these few words, either you will believe or you won't. Whose report do you believe? God's or that other fellow's? The road may be long, but the choice of what direction only takes a second—go ahead, think it over, we've got time—I hope.

# 6.2 TRILLION DOLLAR QUESTION

The 6.2 trillion dollar question represents all the money taxpayers have spent on entitlement programs. Are our fellow citizens stronger or weaker, free or enslaved, happy or miserable? Is there an atmosphere of positivism of the future or a negative one? The thing you Libs "act" like you don't understand is that throwing material (money) things on a spiritual problem is like throwing gasoline on a fire. The two will soon be out of control. I know you guys want to pay the cost (with other people's money). To be the boss, the problem is that human beings have a spiritual side which must be addressed, White, Hispanic or Black. In order to get something out of life, you have to want something out of the life, and what you put into life will determine what you get out of it. The cure to poverty is prosperity. Instead of people in poverty hatin' on people with money, why not try learning how they made it so you can too? I will even start you on the "right" path: 1) work hard; 2) save (time, energy, money); 3) learn (as much as you can/all you need to know); and 4) invest (in yourself, business or good people). If you follow these four principles, how can you go "left" (wrong)?

Give me an "F," give me an "A," give me an "I," give me an "R," give me a "T," give me an "A," give me an "X." What does that spell? Fair Tax! What does that spell, Fair Tax, yeah!! Fair Tax. In order for the plantations and sub-culture to catch up with America to any substantial degree, I think we need to think outside the box. It's true we need to help support the world economies, yet we cannot neglect to support our fellow Americans who need gainful employment. The Fair Tax plan sounds like a good way to revitalize our manufacturing and industrial base. There has to be a happy medium, after all prosperity starts at home...

# RETALIATION

Even though the Bible says, "For it is written, vengeance is mine; I will repay, saith the Lord" (Romans 12:19), the following is my response to what the Libs have been saying against our troops and nation and President and Christians. It, in fact, is my version of an olive branch of peace to try and heal our nation (pay no attention to the big club behind my back). By a show of hands, how many people in America have found their purpose and/or destiny in and for life? One out of 1, 5, 10, 100, 1,000, 100,000, 1,000,000, etc.? Have you found yours? What thing in life brings you fulfillment and satisfaction? The thing that makes work feel like a breeze, and makes you smile for no reason. It excites you, motivates you, and makes you feel "alive!" Have you figured it out yet or are you just drifting aimlessly trying to make it another day caught in a web of mediocrity and futility and vanity? Does this sound familiar?

How many things can you name in nature (God created) or man made that does not have a purpose, a reason for being. Do you really want to live your whole life and not know why you were put here? Even the dirt has a purpose—to be walked on. You would not allow anyone to walk on you and build an empire on you, would you? Or how a simple little match can be used to light a pilot which heats the gas in a furnace, which in turn heats an entire house (empire). Or that same little match can be used to burn down that same house. I guess it all depends on how you use your fire (potential). If every part of your body, nose, eyes, arms, legs, heart, brain, etc.—right down to every cell has a purpose, don't you think you should have one too? By a show of hands, let me know.

In case some of you were wondering, well what is my purpose in life, the thing that animates my world and gives me hope for a brighter future? Take a guess. Give up? You probably knew it was the deconstruction of the Socialist regressive Liberal Democratic Party. Who knew? I was clueless for over 40 years, and then it hit me like a bolt from the blue. Whether they change their names or not, as long as any American is telling his fellow American to be weak, lazy and stupid, I'll be there.

# MORE THINGS TO CONSIDER

1. The one thing Americans need to understand about the nature and power of weakness is the more you give "it," the more it wants. The stronger weakness becomes, the weaker your strength becomes, plus it is very contagious. An example is the Libs trying to appease all their different factions such as fems, gays, baby killers, pacifists, atheists, and Blacks (which, by the way, happen to be the only nationality to support these losers). Or how the Libs drain strength from the Republicans with all their whining and lying and crying; it will drive you crazy if you let it. Or how about those radical fellows who just blow things up to get their way.

2. How far could you, or would you, have gone in life had your own weakness not held you back? The clock is still ticking tick-tock, tick-tock. Better get a move on.

3. The Libs don't think the absolute truth exists. They think it is relative to how they felt at that point and time. That is the major reason why they can't make up their minds for very long. When their feelings change, their mind changes. It's okay to change your mind, but that does not change the truth. That is why we can't let them anywhere near our national security or our constitution, i.e. Liberal judges.

4. I beg to differ. All of the talk radio hosts seem to think the Right is driving the Libs crazy. I don't think you can drive a person to where they already reside (at least not so quickly anyway). An empty suit or skirt, a pretty or handsome face does not a sane person make.

5. Libs don't bother sending your pound-puppy press nipping at the President's heels to try to cause a backlash or to make me heel. I'm a full grown rottweiler. I don't actually work for the President, even though I support him and the troops. When my master tells me sit, I sit. When he tells me roll over, I roll over. But when he tells me sic 'em, at that point it's out of my "paws." I'm just kidding—you

161

Libs need to laugh a little—woof, woof!

6.  Libs, my attacks are not actually aimed at you, so don't take it personally or religiously. It's spiritual, so if nobody moves, nobody gets hurt.

7.  Since Libs don't believe in absolute truth this means they don't believe in God. They are their own individual gods (demi-gods). In fact, they must hate Him because not to believe He exists and holds the truth in His hands is going to invariably set them in opposition to Him, with little or no room for repentance or compromise (as far as admitting you're wrong and starting up the road to His house—the longest journey begins with the first step.)

8.  Since Libs don't understand or accept the truth, they can't understand or accept themselves and their limitations. This is why they are so passive and appeasing towards others who are as lost as they are, but scornfully intolerant of anyone who stands up for the truth, i.e. Christians.

9.  This is why, believers, you may as well get ready for a battle they can't stop nor can we. All mankind are the members of a chess board in the game of life.

10. To the fat cat Libs who sit behind the scenes and pull strings, why are your mouthpieces stuttering and stammering so much when they speak? They sound nervous. Is it because they know that they are lying or causing troops to be in harm's way longer than necessary? Dean, Kerry, Martha Fuller Clark, the women sound much more professional. It figures.

11. The Libs are making too much spiritual chatter. I hope they are not trying to wake up a sleeper cell for their sakes, and for all our sakes.

12. The Republicans in D.C. could take a few spiritual lessons at the "School of mackin'" on how to deal with an unruly broad.

13. The lie is a formula for failure; the truth a formula for success. There are formulas (recipes) for success and formulas for failure. There are roads that lead to peace, and roads that lead to destruction. There is a door that swings both ways on one side, the road to success, on the other side, the road to destruction.

# THE DESTROYER OF CIVILIZATIONS

The gateway to the abyss implosion—to burst or cause to burst inward. Have you ever seen in real life or the news when a building is imploded? Charges are placed on the inside of the building to make it fall down or collapse on itself. The explosives that are placed at a few key locations inside the structure can destabilize the whole building, sending it crashing to the ground. The reason for this analogy is because it is identical to what happens to a man or woman, race or nation, when it or they become enveloped in a chronic case of self-pity, which is right next to pride. Self-pity is the most destructive force known to the human experience, even as pride is an overstatement of self. Self-pity is an understatement of self. In order to fully de-construct this spiritual disease, I would have to write a separate book. Yet, I will try and shed some insight into its destructive power.

Every human being has unlimited potential, which is expressed in the fact that the more you do a certain thing, the better you become at it. The more math you do, the better you become at math; the same for reading, writing, a job, a sport, or a hobby. Positive potential is always expressed outward, everything from the words of your mouth, to the tree in the seed, to a woman giving birth, to grass growing out of the ground, to the sun in the sky shining down on us, which gives us the heat, light and energy we need to live a healthy life here on earth. In fact, your life is a lot like the sun, when you are healthy and happy; you project light, heat and energy to people around you. Yet on the other hand, for some reason whether upbringing, environment, culture, doctrine, political ideology, or medical or psychological disorder, you become a person who is always feeling sorry for himself. That's when, instead of you being about life and all it has to offer, you indulge in self pity. Life starts to be about you, which is backwards; it should come to you to take care of you—in a word, selfish. This spiritual disorder can happen to a person, race, religion, or nation. If the implosion is not closed a vortex will open in your soul that will never be satisfied. The more you get, the weaker you will become, which will manifest in the form of a sense of low self-esteem, low self-respect, and low self-worth. At that point, you give yourself over to all manner of bad habits, i.e. cigarettes, drugs, alcohol, crime, violence, lying, cheating, stealing, fighting, all manner of hatred, anger, jealousy, self-loathing, and self-defeating. Every manner of negative thing happens when a person pities himself for too long. Self pity is pure weakness turned inward. It will destroy you if you let it. At the core of pity is a lie, that you can't be strong, independent and happy—which is what God has planned for your life. If you are an introvert, you tend to only hurt yourself. If you are an extrovert, you tend to hurt other people.

The cure for self pity is the truth, and the truth is just that. The world does not revolve around you, so get over yourself and start giving back to life. It is more blessed to give than to receive.

Those are just a few reasons not to fall into this destructive habit. Always count your blessings and walk the sunny side of the street.

Now that you see self pity for what it is, no healthy person in their right mind would have anything to do with it. Why would they intentionally pollute and destroy their own life for no good reason? Well, I'm sorry to say that there are people who actually project self pity on other people to gain control over their lives—whether they need to be pitied or not. If you tell someone something long enough, they will start to believe it. For instance, if someone tells your race that they are disenfranchised victims who need to be protected and cared for, they will begin to believe it and start to act on what they believe. This is what the Lib Dems have done to the Black race in America. They have used psy-ops to brainwash 90% of Blacks to believe lies for the purpose for securing a voter base.

The Lib Dems are Socialists which means they think government should be the center of your world, not you, not God. They want to tell you what to do, how to do it, where, and when. Socialism is government induced self pity through welfare and entitlement programs. They control your life, not you. You have to pay the cost to be the boss.

Blacks will never be free in this country until we cut the apron strings. The twin sister to Socialism is Liberalism, which is culturally induced self pity. When people are already feeling down and out, they tend to choose the path of least resistance, i.e. crime, drugs, sexual immorality, alcohol abuse, partying, etc. They are trying to escape the misery and futility of being stuck and not going anywhere in life because they have given up control of their lives for a few dollars. Dignity for dollars. There is nothing wrong with getting help if you really need it to get on your feet. But to think someone owes you a free ride through life is a joke being played on you by you.

# THE VORTEX

Through lies, deceit and projecting self pity, the Libs have opened up a spiritual, political, and cultural vortex of weakness and self pity that is draining the life, resources and potential out of everyone caught in it.

The vortex has been open for about 40 years, and it's still growing. Since the Libs own the culture, news, movies, music, T.V., clothes, schools, and colleges, they control most of what you see, hear and learn. The Libs have packaged immorality in such a neat, cool, pretty, sexy, and tough container, that kids are falling for it hook, line and sinker. When they open the box, they get blown into the event horizon (E.H.)—talk about a smart bomb or I.E.D. Once you land in the E.H., time begins to stand still, in that people begin to tell themselves everything is okay and that they will get back on track tomorrow or the next day, all the while the people who are stuck there with you are telling you, "Let's party and hang out and look cool,, tough, sexy, etc." In real time the clock is ticking.

Next thing you know 1, 5, 10, 15, 20, 30, 40, 50, 60 years have passed and you wasted your whole life on nothing—mindless sex, drugs, parties, clothes, etc. All of these things are not worth a hill of beans in the long run. If you ever saw the movie *The Matrix* it's like the scene that showed a lot of people in cocoons being drained of their life's energy, all the while dreaming that they were living. That's what your life will be like without the truth in it. Wake up, and you'll find that you've been dreaming. If you think cars, jewelry, illicit sex, illegal drugs, money, motorcycles, fame, etc. is all that matters in life, or that they make you who you really are, they don't. Only God can tell you who you are; after all He made you!

## THE SOLUTION

Now if all the thousands and thousands of hours of watching sci-fi movies are ever going to pay off, it is now. The truth is the only force that can close a spiritual vortex of weakness.

If I were to take this chapter and package it, which is equivalent to a 330 megaton spiritual nuclear device, and drop it into the mainstream conservative party, people would begin to get excited about it, and pass it around to everyone they knew realizing this would be a great chance to save this nation from splitting in two. This would be the fusion generation stage with the Internet, talk radio, and blog-o-sphere. The Right could reach critical mass stage in a year or less. Then at 95% critical mass, they would send a positive shock wave of truth into the vortex—you are an American, a unique individual. Don't waste the only life you will get by being full of self pity and weakness. Do your best to be your best, and share that with the world. Even if you are poor, you can still have class and dignity; some people with money have neither.

Theoretically, the longer we keep the truth focused on the vortex, the truth will cause the vortex to de-stabilize. It will weaken and people will be able to escape and get back what's left of their lives. We could go back 10, 20, 30, 40 years to the time when the split began. Then we could make a right turn instead of a left, and be on the right track again. And for those who are not into sci-fi, this concept is strikingly similar to a husband and wife. Hey, we are all adults here. I know that this analogy sounds corny to a degree. I only used it to explain the way the nation is being pulled into darkness and what we need to do to stop it. There are lives at stake, after all, not to mention our kids and their kids.

P.S.    I believe the Russians have a weapon that emits a large electromagnetic pulse wave that knocks out all electrical appliances in a given area. The terrorists are said to be seeking it. This is the same principle: except one is spiritual, the other electrical.

# AMERICA: FIGHT OR FLIGHT?

Although America has answered the call to battle against radical terrorists in Iraq, there is another war and another battle being waged on our borders. The war in the states has four fronts, spiritual, political, cultural, and economical. The war is actually spiritual, yet the conservatives do not know how to fight this kind of foe, because it is a battle of ideologies—morals, ethics, truth, lies, desires, etc. For the most part, the Right has been either barely holding the line or downright running away. This is why the Leftist movement is still growing. To fight or flee; America is going to have to face this adversary sooner or later.

There was one other time in American history when we had to battle each other, the Civil war. As I said before, everything emanates from the spiritual realm. The war for now is emotional versus mental. If America will but wake up and stand, we can spare ourselves a lot of heartache and misery. It is hard to believe that history is repeating itself and at the heart of the matter once again is slavery. If Blacks would wake up, we might be able to avoid the oncoming disaster. Wake up America (alarm clock sounding). Wake up honey! It is time to get up! Wake up sweetie America! You are going to miss your date with destiny. Now, get up!!!

I hope the Right is not afraid to stand their ground and face the truth, and then act on it. I mean secular and religious have to put their differences aside, and be ready to hear the Left lie, cry, whine and bitch. They will use political correctness (social terrorism) to make you feel sorry for them, so as to not hurt their feelings. Remember they are already weak-minded, and anything you say as far as the truth is concerned will hurt their feelings. Don't listen.

I wrote this chapter to explain where we are and what we need to do. Just let people read and decide for themselves. I think it is the best way. If the blog-o-sphere, Internet providers and talk radio won't let the Left "punk" them out, then we have a fighting chance. If they start to yell "separation of church and state" or some other such rubbish, tell them this material is spiritual, not religious, and since man is 90% spirit, you can't separate him from the truth and the life he lives. You will not overcome your adversary if you don't face your adversary.

# THE MANTLE

I consider the landscape of our nation's past, present, and future in respect to the three generations that are now here. Together "The Great Generation" held the line and taught us about valor, courage, honor, integrity, love, and morals. They taught us that family friends and country are worth fighting for and if need be, dying for. We can't thank them enough. Yet, as they move into the past, the mantle has been placed in our hands to keep the light of liberty illuminating the path of truth, not for America only, but for the world as well.

We have been given an awesome responsibility not to be taken for granted or taken lightly. We here in the present are faced with a daunting task as to how to keep this nation from being torn in two. I think this can be accomplished, but we will have to move fast and be strong. In my opinion, as I survey our future, I think that our backs are against the wall. The reason I say this is because the future generation has been inundated with immoral attitudes and behavior. They seem to be overly sensitive, addicted to pleasure and comfort; they tend to be lazy, obese, rebellious, and violent. Looking at the poor test scores, criminal behavior, school drop-outs, teen abortions/pregnancies, alcohol and drug abuse, depression, suicidal and over-medicated, this seems painfully clear.

They have very little knowledge of the truth or how important it is to human development and survival. For these reasons and many more, the buck must stop here! We cannot afford to pass this headache onto our offspring. They may not be able to handle it. If we can't face the truth and they know less than we do, then America is in trouble. He who stands for nothing will fall for anything.

# THE CONDUCTOR

As I consider the upcoming title fight for a nation between Queen Lib and America, I think it might be better for me to stay underground, because no one person can save a country. All of my fellow Americans who actually love America have to stand up and beat the heck out of the Lib queen. This is not about the color of the skin, black or white, but the color of the heart. Whether male or female, young or old, rich or poor, religious or secular, all the people who believe in America, its morality and freedom need to stand up as one with a loud voice and tell the Lib queen to take a hike off a short cliff. We shall see. "Let's get ready to R-u-m-b-l-e!" I wonder if I could get some action from the bookies in Vegas. Will America fight or take flight? If America keeps running, then I guess I will just contact the conductor of the Underground Railroad and see if he's got a spare bunk on his train. I can travel across country helping as many escape the plantation as possible.

In this way I can continue to eat all the pancakes I want in peace. Even though I only have a high school education, I find all of the Libs I talk to and the ones I hear on the news to be terribly dishonest, ignorant and weak-minded, all of them. They all say the same thing as though they were suspiciously under control of one mind—the lawyers, politicians, the judges, the foot soldiers—all sound just alike. It leads me to believe that in their effort to deny the truth they have or are driving themselves insane. There is no use talking to them because there's nothing there. The lights are on, but nobody's home.

If you were sitting around with nothing better to do and thought about the different factions of the Left, you would see fat cats behind the scenes pulling strings like a puppet master afraid to come out in the open. The politicians in D.C. are little spoiled brats, who are stark raving mad because they are out of power and will say anything to regain power, even put our troops in harm's way by giving aid and comfort to the enemy, just like Vietnam. They are like twelve year old evil little rascals in suits and skirts; Spanky, Alfalfa, Darla, Worm, Chubby, Froggy, Butch, Buckwheat, Stymie, Little Mickey, Waldo, Ms. Crabtree, Wheezer

172

and Farina. Yup, the whole gang's all here. Then there are the feminists who want to turn the society from patriarchal to matriarchal. Totally ass backwards. They are full of hate and anger against men.

Then the baby killers, they hate life altogether. Then the men who love men, and women who love women. Since you don't need sex to live, then this abnormal behavior is perverted and dangerous and contagious to a normal society. Then there are the people who believe that someone has nothing better to do than to hold them back, when they are doing a perfectly good job of it on their own. The only people trying to hold them back are the people they are following.

If we were to look at the Left as one collective mind, what would you see them manifest? Hate, lust, murder, violence, perversity, power hungry, extremely selfish, egotistical, self-centered, maniacal, overly emotional, self-pitying, unforgiving, and vengeful. Are these the type of people you want to have control of this country? Well, do you?

## THE LIST

"<u>Has Been</u>" (HB) = Person or thing whose popularity has past.

HB List: Martha, McCain, Clark—please take a seat and fade into the past.

## BLACK REPUBLICANS

Greetings in the name of the Truth. Even though I have only been a conservative for a short time, I know it's where I belong.

They say we only make up 10% of the Black vote to the right side of the aisle. I don't believe this is accurate. There are more of us that are conservative and just don't know it. Our job is to find those that are, and by the time of the next election we should shoot for 50%.

Let's look at the 10%. We are either useless, or we are sitting at a pivotal point in our nation's history and can make a real difference in the future of this nation. No guts, no glory. Know guts, know glory.

If we are only 10% and the rest is 90%, then I ask you which way is up because I'm told the cream always rises to the top, so where are you?

The Lord usually gives notice before He shakes things up like Jonah and the City of Nineveh. He fires a warning shot to let people know that the handwriting on the wall needs to be read and acted on. Ignoring the handwriting will not stop it from coming to past. So let's stop studying and preaching about the past events of the Bible. Those people are always learning, but never knowing the power of the truth. If you want to know where God is, He is in the ever present, millisecond of positive energy of right now for anyone who is ready to stand up for the truth and take action. That's where God is.

P.S.    In the spiritual realm, there's a whole lotta' shakin' going on. Can you feel it? Can you smell what the Lord is cooking?

# WHERE ARE OUR MANNERS?

To the best of my knowledge, no one has taken the opportunity to officially welcome, on behalf of the God of America, all the Muslims who have come to this country to live, work and raise families in these borders of the United States. I would also, if I may be so bold to, say on behalf of our God that He loves you very much. Not only Muslims, but people from all different religions and walks of life. His desire is for men of all different colors, races, creeds, and cultures to come together and live in harmony as one. America is the place He has chosen for this great human experiment. We welcome you to make all of the positive contributions you wish to help America thrive. This is a great country in which to live if you love life. There are so many things to do and learn and see. There is, compared to the rest of the world, prosperity and riches to go around. Only people who are spoiled and take it for granted cannot see how good they have it. They always see the glass as half full. They spend so much time counting other peoples' blessings that they forget to count their own blessings. These people are so suspicious, jealous and unhappy, so full of self-pity, that they are very easy to take advantage of, take control of, brainwash and manipulate.

I understand most Muslims have a big problem with the immorality in America. Well, that's because a group of people who don't like our country have moved in and are using and taking advantage of these unhappy Americans, giving them other people's money, pointing the finger of blame at other people, "Reps", all the while propagating and instigating the cause of their sorrow (immorality). They preach that an immoral lifestyle is the key to freedom, when it is in fact a key to enslavement.

The culprits are the Liberal Democrats in D.C. and a few other choice organizations. The rest of the "Dems" still think that the Libs are the party of the working man. That is what they were in the 1960s, but now they are Socialists who want the government to have almost complete control over your life. So if you Muslims in America would like to continue to enjoy the peace and prosperity of America, I invite you to make a stand for morality and let your

176

voices be heard. If your god is the God of peace and our God is love, then there should be no room for disagreement between our people. Let us put all infidels to flight that we may all see our sons and daughters live and grow strong, that we may see good all our days and eat the fat of the land.

It should be quite obvious that the people on the Right have the love of God in them because the President has sent troops to liberate your fellow Muslims in Iraq. Over 25 million of your brethren will have a chance to govern themselves and be free to control their own destiny as God intended. We Americans have laid down our lives, white, black, brown and yellow to accomplish this. Not only to liberate them, but to protect us here at home. We in the USA Right are a peace loving people who love and cherish the life our God has given us, however we will lay it down for the cause of freedom and to protect our loved ones in this country. The world would be a much better place to live if weak-minded people all over the world would find the courage to stop feeling sorry for themselves, to stop being so selfish, and to stop trying to protect their own lives. The fear of losing their life is what gives tyrants and dictators control over them to keep them in bondage. He who seeks to save his life will lose it; he who loses his life for the truth's sake will find it.

It would be great if some of our fellow Muslims would speak out for peace in the Middle East. Who knows, you might go down in history as a great man or woman in the history of your religion and the world.

Speaking as a Black man in this country, my race was not born free in this nation, but our God has brought us out so that we can have everything we set our minds to accomplish. The only way anyone can hold you back is if you agree with them. This is the only life we all have to live. Why waste it? Look at your little children and consider the type of life you wish for them to have. It's up to us.

Even though there are some who have determined in themselves to die in order to obtain victory, we have determined in ourselves to live to obtain the same. May God have mercy on us all. Amen.

# FEMME FATALE

To the spirit of the feminist movement, on behalf of all the old-timers back in the day who took you for granted, who neglected you, who did not appreciate you, and who had you slave over a hot stove with a bun in the oven and one on the hip. I apologize. They should have been more appreciative and thankful for the help-mate that God gave man. There is no excuse for this behavior. They were just a bunch of meanies. Having said that, I think now would be a good time for you ladies to take a serious look at the trickle down effect of the sexual revolution you launched back in the '60s. The spiritual, emotional, intellectual and physical damage is catastrophic, to put it mildly. I don't know whether you knew what you were doing at the time, but you have all but brought this nation to its spiritual knees at a time when we can least afford to be weak.

Those of you at the top of the Liberal Democratic Party should come and spend some time down here at the bottom and see what a nightmare you have created—all for a voter base. Whether you knew it or not, ignorance of the law is no excuse.

The young women whom you claim to represent, the ones whom you told to disrespect themselves in regard to their bodies and sex, are now having their God-given and tender hearts <u>crushed</u>!!! emotionally, physically, mentally and spiritually.

I have met so many women who have been abused, mistreated and abandoned, even as little girls by deadbeat dads, and as grown women with a lot of baggage. It is a wonder they have not gone insane. I meet women who don't even like men anymore, except for sexual intercourse, and women who are starting to like women more and more. And there are young women who even like to be abused by men; referred to as "roughnecks." I see women who feel so bad about themselves they won't let you treat them nice, they want to be treated according to the way they feel about themselves, which is bad (low self-esteem). Now they will never be a housewife or anything else God might have had for them. Not to mention disease; HIV/AIDS and other STD's are almost at epidemic proportions on the plantations and in the sub-culture. Far too many men are like little boys in a candy store, they can't decide whether they want light or dark chocolate or caramel or a cream puff or honey bun. Just like a kid in a toy store, they do not know if they want a remote controlled Hummer, a nice 'Vette, or something that's good on curves. They think it makes them more of a man to have lots of women, but it actually makes them less of a man. They lose the three attributes that define any man. These attributes are responsibility, respect and discipline. I see some guys that are so fem they think it's manly to make a woman buy them things and take care of them. And some women are so desperate they will neglect their own kids to buy a grown man a suit, jewelry, shoes, etc. These are just a few of the dysfunctional conditions that have been spawned because of the sexual revolution.

There are so many problems to deal with, especially with the little kids who will never have the benefit of a mother and father in the home. According to God, the father is the center and main support for the family. He is the protector and covering for his wife. He is the first man his daughter will set as her role model for the type of man she will be attracted to. The father is the one to teach his son the first thing he will be when he grows up as a man. The three attributes of respect, responsibility and discipline.

There are many fathers who are not in the home and far too many young girls and women who are wearing clothes two to three sizes too small for them, just to get attention from a man. This will only cause a man to see them as an object and not a person, which will put them in the same position that their parents put them in. This cycle has to be broken.

The young boys are also being neglected, without a father to teach them the meaning of hard work, morals, and values. They are picking up guns to prove their manhood, joining gangs, and taking other people's lives over a few drugs or money. They have no self worth at all. They think "to get rich or die trying" is all that is worth living and dying for.

You Liberals have so much blood on your hands for promoting

immorality in this country. When all the accounts are settled, I would not want to be you for all the sex, drugs, money, power or pleasure in the world.

Socialism and Liberalism are completely and totally utter failures. You need to abandon those politics and lifestyles as soon as possible. This is just a word to the wise.

Oh, and that's not to mention all the unwanted pregnancies and abortions. You ladies of the feminist movement put Freddy Krueger to shame. If I were you—if you knew like I know—I would repent as fast as possible and try to stop this scourge before it gets any worse. Don't be angry with me because I care enough about you to tell you the truth. Two wrongs will not make a right.

Well, well, well!! Well, well, well!! This is a fine kettle of fish you guys have gotten us into. The founding fathers had to go and invoke the God of Abraham, Isaac and Jacob to lay the spiritual foundation for the framework of the nation. And if that was not enough, they used biblical principles to frame the Constitution which has guided America to this place of prominence in world history. If that was not enough, based on God's moral standard, you guys had to set up a system of government, a democratic republic that allows the people by the power of their vote to control the directions of the nation, which is the best way to rule. "Of the people, by the people, for the people."

Well, well, well!! As if you had not done enough, you went and set up a way of doing business called Capitalism which provides the greatest access to the greater number of people to acquire wealth which in turn inspires and creates more wealth. This provides jobs for more Americans to earn a living and take care of their families.

With the combination of God, the Constitution, our form of government, democratic republic and Capitalism, we have created an infrastructure that is second to none. The roads and bridges, the airlines, the postal services, the shops and stores, the water and sewer systems, the banking and monetary systems, the medical and technology industry, the homes, cars, buses, motorcycles, restaurants, parks, libraries, churches, etc. There are more things to do, see, and learn than I can mention, all of which provide Americans with so much freedom and liberty that people risk life and limb to get here (illegally), just to be a part of having a chance of a better life for their families.

There is so much freedom here that people are free to enslave themselves to drugs, sex, alcohol, etc. Go figure. There is so much freedom here to allow people who don't even like our God, our Constitution, our form of government, our business system, to be free to voice their opinion. They are so unintelligent as to not realize that if they make any substantial changes to our way of life, then they jeopardize all that we have been given and obtained by the grace of God. If it ain't broke, then don't fix it!!

As I said before, well, well, well! I hope that you all are very satisfied and happy with yourselves—as well you should be. America is an evolving and shining example of what men and women can accomplish under the moral/spiritual leadership of God.

It is for these reasons and many more that I am writing this book, so as not to lose all the blessings we already have. The Lord has a real problem with ungrateful people. Since when did believing in God make you an extremist? In fact, the opposite is true, if you ask me. People who don't believe in God are extremists.

# CAN YOU HANDLE THE TRUTH?

The Republicans and conservatives are in need of a reality check to see if they can actually handle the truth. The conservatives have had some success in the political arena, but that is no reason to become complacent and to think that the Libs have given up. This is not solely a personal struggle or a political struggle. This is more than a generational struggle. This is a spiritual struggle, therefore it is an eternal struggle. There are people on both sides of the battle who are not here anymore, yet the battle rages on.

If the "Cons" (conservatives) want to get serious about winning this battle, they are going to have to find the courage to stand up to and face the Libs in the open light of day. They are going to have to stop preaching to the choir and make headway into the Lib base, i.e. the sub-culture and spiritual plantations. The Libs are making progress with your kids via schools, colleges, and the culture, i.e. music, movies, video games, rap videos, etc. The best way to keep your opponent off your tail is to stay on his. The Cons are going to have to stand up, take the gloves off, and tell the truth, whatever the cost or loss. There is going to be a backlash from the main stream media, sort of like your kid when you tell them they are grounded. So what, get over it!! The thing you Cons need to accept is that the "Lib queen" has an agenda. The days of good old spirited debate are over for now.

The Lib queen is a lot like the babe in *Terminator 3* (but not as cute). She does not care what you say, think, feel, act, want, or do. She will not veer from her agenda ever. She will say, do, or act anyway she has to in order to get you to compromise your position. She will change her shape or form in any number of ways, e.g. A.C.L.U., most unions, sexual orientations, races, religions, civil rights leaders, political leaders, and college professors, but all have the same agenda, the fall of America.

Have you ever heard your dad tell you, "If you play with yourself, you will go blind?" Well it's true, if you play with the Lib queen as if she was your friend or if you believe that she cares about you or this country, you have gone blind.

I had a recent girlfriend whom I cared about greatly, but when the truth came out, I was just playing with myself because I refused to read the handwriting on the wall. We can't afford to make the same mistake with America.

Some of the Republicans in Washington (D.C.) are already falling into the vortex of weakness. The vortex is similar to a spiritual leach. It converts strength to weakness. Whether we are winning at the poles or not, the vortex is still open and the transfusion from morality to immorality is still taking place so it will eventually amount to a problem deferred with interest.

Because of what the "Queen" has done to my race (although everyone is responsible for his or her actions), by intentionally deceiving those people who were already struggling to find an identity (vulnerable), those parties guilty of this act are complicit in the ensuing demise of said race.

This is the reason I personally have some bones to pick and some axes to grind, and I do mean GRIND!!

In case I have to pull a Cindy Sheehan, I have my "tell the truth, free the slaves" signs ready to go. As I asked before, "can you handle the truth?" If you can and you are married with children, then look into your kids' eyes and see their hope for the future and make a promise to yourself to help them meet it. Then in 60 seconds or less, give your wife a kiss that will make her see stars and stripes, make her weak in the knees so much so that she turns into a gentle mist of love, and gently floats back upstairs to keep your bed warm for you only. Then grab your spiritual guts, gear and glory and run out to meet your unit, to keep your family safe. And if you can't handle the truth, keep sitting there playing with yourself and continue to go blind. You are dismissed!!

P.S.    If you are single like me, save your valor for the battlefield. Drink black coffee from a tin cup, and take a bite of Jerky, if you have it. If not, peel some bark off a tree, we are the rough necks.

## MORAL EQUIVALENCE

Have you ever considered these two words as I have after hearing them bandied about by the Libs? They actually make no sense at all. Since the word moral has a wide range of thoughts, feelings, and actions which in turn lead to a host of situations and circumstances ranging from positive to negative, and a great number in between. The spectrum is from morality to immorality so there never, ever, could be a moral equivalence. That would be like saying Mother Theresa and Hitler were on the same page, or the troops and the terrorists were on the same page. Then why are they fighting? That's like saying the justice league and the legion of doom are of the same ilk. Most reprehensible of all is like saying Jesus and Satan are in agreement over the state of humanity. That's like punching, slapping and spitting in His face, like they did on His way to the cross.

# LIB UPDATE

Libs don't actually love life or America. They love the things in them, e.g. pleasure, money, sex, and power/control, which are essentially the slow road to self-destruction. Liberalism is not only a mental disorder, but a spiritual disorder as well. Talking to someone who does not believe that there is truth in the universe is like talking to the wind. You never now which way it will blow next. To Libs civil rights equals civil selfishness, which equals civil self-pity, which equals civil unrest. Libs are fearful of what they see in themselves, and they project it onto others, i.e. Patriot Act, war in Iraq. They are the ones who would unlawfully spy on their fellow Americans or exploit Iraq for their oil. To the pure, all things are pure, to the unclean, all things are unclean. Since Libs don't actually believe there is a God that is superior to how they think or feel in their hearts that makes them equal to God, sort of like that other fellow who got tossed out for thinking such foolishness. And that's why they all think it is their job to bring humanity under control, i.e. Socialism, Communism, radical Muslims. The sad thing is they are fighting a battle that has already been lost and won.

I know some of you tender-hearted Libs and some Cons may think I'm over the top, a radical, an extremist. If you believe that, then all I can ask you is how much is America worth to you? How much! How much! How much!!! When battling an adversary like this, it is imperative that you be faster, wiser, stronger and hit harder than they do—so sticks and stones may break my bones, but names will never hurt me! Nark, nark, nark.

Since self pity is the glue that holds all the factions of the Liberal Democratic Party together, and since they are all unhappy people, is it any wonder that self pity equals misery and misery loves company? I do have some good news for the Libs that have read this chapter up to this point. Before you read it, we were worlds apart. Now that you have read it, you are in my mind and my mind is in you. It's a beautiful day in the neighborhood.

In case anyone is interested in how I have drawn my conclusions,

185

the Bible says that all men are born into sin (weakness). Well, I like you, was born into sin, plus I was born spiritually blind (I had no sense of self). So not only was I born in weakness, according to the Bible I was also born in spiritual darkness, therefore I was farther left than the majority of you Leftists. (I know your pain.)

You cannot imagine the pain and confusion of being blind and weak. Most people in this state usually go crazy, commit suicide, become drug addicts, alcoholics, sex addicts or eat themselves to death. To medicate the pain, you will do just about anything.

I spent 40 years being torn apart emotionally, spiritually, mentally and physically. The only thing that got me through is I had a teacher who stayed with me. He said he would never leave me nor forsake me (Deuteronomy 31:6). He stayed closer than a brother (Proverbs 18:24). His favorite word was "again"—do it over again, try again, over and over. I had to learn to see in the dark, then to see weakness. I had to learn who was in the spiritual darkness, what their purpose was, and who sent them. I had to learn how the darkness moves from person to person, and in one's self. I was far left of most of you. If I thought you had a snow ball's chance in hell, I might be able to understand (psych). Everything goes back to where it came from, ashes to ashes, dust to dust. All weakness (people included) that for whatever reason (self pity) rejects the truth will have hell to pay with their eternal soul. You are playing Russian roulette with a two barrel revolver.

I am not some stuffed shirt, uptight, unfeeling, insensitive, conservative who cannot understand what it's like to be you, to hurt for days, weeks, months, and years. God allowed me to be acquainted with pain beyond measure. So I can relate.

Wouldn't you like to know what it feels like to be whole? That means your thoughts, feelings, and actions are all in agreement with what is best for you. No drugs, no alcohol, no unmarried sex.

# THIS IS YOUR LIFE

That was the name of a popular television documentary series back in the '50s where the contestants had to guess the identity of the person from his or her past who helped shape his life, i.e. a friend, teacher or classmate, etc. The reason I mention the show is that any one of us could either be a contestant, or the other person who helped shape someone's life. The one major difference is that *This Is Your Life* was a staged show, which is not the case with real life.

This book was written with love for every American in this country, legal or illegal. The most important and priceless thing you possess is your life. As far as I know, we all only get one. One chance to express all of who we are and what we would hope to achieve. What do you think the purpose of life is? What is (or could be) your purpose or mission in this life we share? Do you think it is to be the best of all you can be, the least/worst you can be, or to be neutral and blend into mediocrity like everybody else?

In my humble opinion after over 40 years of life, I believe the purpose of this life is to give us the opportunity to do all we can to be the best we can be. Apparently this is not as easy or simple to achieve as it sounds or else everyone would be doing it. Why is it that some people live happy, fulfilling, successful lives and others live lives of torment, shame, and emptiness? And for that matter what constitutes a successful life versus a failed one, aside from the obvious of someone having fame and fortune, versus someone who is poor and unpopular? These two seem to be the parameters upon which we in this country and most of the world judge each other. Yet on closer observation, after you look past the surface, it is plain to see that people with fame and fortune are sometimes miserable, lonely and angry people. Likewise there are people who are poor and relatively unknown who are happy and content with their lives. Also there are people in prison who enjoy more freedom than people who are walking the streets today. So what is it that we can conclude from these facts about life? 1) That money and fame don't guarantee happiness and contentment, but can actually lead to your demise due to a false sense of reality; 2) your physical surroundings (environment) do not dictate the amount of success or freedom a person may enjoy in life. Based on these conclusions, we can clearly see that there is a recipe, a formula for successful living and a recipe or formula for a failed life.

With all the complexities of modern life, how do we keep the world inside your head and mine sane, versus the one we all share with everyone else that presently has life in them? One formula is the truth; it works no matter who tries it. The other formula is untrue (lies), no matter whom or how many use it. I think it is obvious to see that a successful life is a positive life, and an unsuccessful life is a negative one. So what is the truth, and what is the definition of a successful life? There are three worlds (realms) that we all interact with in life. There is the inner world of your heart and mind—expressed in your thoughts and feelings, which manifests itself in your words and actions in this ($2^{nd}$) physical world we share. And the third, which is actually the primary realm, is the spiritual realm (God's realm) which you are connected to through your mind and heart. That is where your ideas, beliefs, and feelings emanate from.

Everything that man has created or invented originated in his mind, which is connected to the spiritual realm—books, music, cars, planes, buildings, homes, appliances, governments, laws, etc. Likewise everything in the universe, including you, existed in God's mind before He created it and you. So it stands to reason to live a truly successful life, you must position yourself in the truth so that all three realms are being positively affected by you. The Bible sums this task up in this way, "You shall love the Lord thy God with all thy mind, heart, body and soul, and the second commandment is as the first. You shall love your neighbor (fellow man) as you love yourself" (Deuteronomy 6:5, Leviticus 19:18).

As I stated in the beginning of this chapter, this book is all about you and your life. The following question is the most important one anyone has ever asked you at any time in your life. <u>Do you love yourself spiritually, intellectually, emotionally and physically?</u> Since real love is pure, positive, whole and infinite, do the four aspects of your being function as one (being whole)? Do your thoughts, words, feelings, and deeds (actions) stem from a positive or negative source? If you are like most people, you are fragmented in your soul. In other words, if you don't love God with all of your being and might, then you can't actually love yourself. You know that positivism is good, but do you spend time thinking on negative or destructive thoughts? The same for feelings, whether they be against God, yourself or others. How much time do you spend being negative? What about your words and actions? How much time do you spend disrespecting God, yourself, and your fellow man? Since life is like a living mirror, it will only show you what you see in yourself. If you love yourself and want a successful life, why would you spend your time mistreating yourself? If you think, feel, act, and speak in negative ways, they will only come back to you (not to mention ticking off God and your fellow man). If you love yourself, why would you do drugs, abuse alcohol, overeat, smoke cigarettes, and worst of all give yourself to someone sexually that you are not married to? Because each time you do, you fragment the four aspects of your being. Besides disobeying God, anyone can see all the destructiveness caused by diseases, abortions, illegitimate children, etc.

Do you love yourself? If you don't love yourself, how can you like yourself? The only way you can do this is, is if you or someone has deceived you into thinking it's strong to be weak. To think it's positive to be negative, to be wrong and think you are right, to be dishonest and think you are honest, and when you couple all of this deception with thoughts and feelings of hate, lust, envy, fear, pride, apathy, unforgiveness, selfishness, laziness, greed, and self pity. Just from these few words you can see what a hopeless dilemma man is in, without the power of His Holy Spirit. To have a whole and successful life according to the purpose for which He created us. Since we do live in a fallen world with a negative force at work, some people end up in some really bad and painful situations, and some are born with them. Yet God can take any person and situation and turn it into a blessing, if we only trust and obey.

# GOING THROUGH THE MOTIONS

"How's life treating you?" That used to be the greeting people would use in the old days, back in the '70s. Yet in my observation, a more accurate greeting would be "How are you treating life?"

So up to this point, what can we conclude about a successful life and as to whether or how much you love yourself? I think we can say that in order to have a successful life, you must try to make progress in order to move forward in life in a positive direction; to explode into the future to make a way for yourself and your family. To go in reverse would cause an implosion into which you would cave in on yourself and those connected to you. You also could, like most people, just tread water through life. They try to stay lukewarm all the time. Are you living or going through the motions?

As far as the question of do you love yourself according to God, how much could you get accomplished if you were 80% whole spiritually, intellectually, emotionally, and physically? What if 70% of the people in your home, city, and state were 70 to 80% positive most of the time (because no one is perfect)? This is what God is looking for, people who want to love Him, themselves and their fellow man. God loves you so much, He wants you to know how well and powerful it feels to be a whole person who is full of the truth, love and life. He believes in what you can do and can be, if you trust Him. It is a shame that some people and forces are hell bent on telling you what you can't do or be. Whose report are you going to believe?

This is why the Lord came to set you free from yourself, this material world and the force of darkness. The Bible says, "He who the Son sets free is free indeed" (John 8:36). The Word also says, "He came that you should have life and have it more abundantly" (John 10:10). The way to receive this new life is you must be born again. This basically means asking God to put His strong, whole, powerful, loving, wise, and full of life Spirit in you. The choice is yours—God's Spirit or your fragmented, negative, weak, and dying spirit. How much life do you have in your living versus how much death do you have in your living?

190

It's your life, it's your call, choose life—spiritual life versus physical life, since everything emanates from the spiritual realm, thoughts, feelings, actions. You are actually going backwards to let the things of the material world come first, such as money, cars, homes, clothes, sex, etc. versus honor, love, respect, discipline, etc. Those other things are yours to have, but what does it profit a man to gain the whole world and lose his own soul? To move backwards in life is a form of spiritual implosion.

The term going out of the world "tail" backwards was used to describe a person who for whatever reason began to implode on himself or herself until at last they die some senseless, tragic death. Everything in the physical and spiritual realms, with life in them, moves upward, outward, and forward.

There is a hurricane of potential inside each of us waiting to be released. The trick is to the degree you believe the truth, you will explode with positivism, and to the degree you believe lies, you will implode with negativity. Then there are the people, like most of us, who at one time or another refused to or could not make up their minds, which causes the middle-of-the-road, straddle the fence, lukewarm mentality. Life itself is actually positive and is meant to be lived that way. Life was not meant to be debated as to whether we should live positive, negative or lukewarm. This you might say is the knowledge between good and evil.

Since death is negative and life is positive, you really can't serve two masters. You will love one and hate the other, or cling to the one and despise the other. The way the system works is that you can't actually do both. If you try you will have a split personality which will lead to a negative life anyway. The sunshine and the dark of night don't share the same space. Albeit for human beings we can deceive ourselves and pretend like we can do both, but eventually it all comes to the surface. So as hard as it is to achieve, learn to choose life in thought, work, feelings, and deeds. Trust Jesus.

# A TALE OF TWO CITIES

Or should I say, two for the price of one. It seems to me that the latter is a more accurate description of the state of our nation today. Starting from the head down to the foot, from politics to religion, to business to culture, we have two Americas; albeit I consider one group real Americans, and the other group U.S. citizens. One group loves the spirit of America (Liberty). The other group includes the lovers of American freedom (L.O.A.F.'ers for short). Both groups come in all different colors, shapes, sizes, sexes, ages, and backgrounds. One group is primarily in a perpetual state of explosion with faith, hope, love, sacrifice, and hard work. The other group is in a perpetual state of implosion with fear, doubt, worry and selfishness. The following is my bottom line assessment of our nation. Some people will be angry and hurt, but some people will be glad and thankful. That fact is a good indication that this is the truth to the best of my ability, yet nevertheless my mission is to save souls from being eternally lost in hell. I would also like to add that since I'm a Black man, I do have racial license to talk about these topics. Also because I am an American as well as a child of God, I have the same license to discuss these subjects as well (just for the record).

The first thing I would like to take issue with is to the Bible scholars and theologians in the framing of the word "weakness" as opposed to the word "sin." I know some of you might think that I'm trying to water down the word of God, but I'm not at all. In my walk with the Lord, I have found that my "sins" are the same as my weaknesses. For whenever I am weak, I sin against God, myself or my fellow man. So don't ever think I would dare alter the word of God to make the impact of "sin" of no effect, for the wages of sin is death—spiritually, intellectually, emotionally and physically. The judgment for being weak (sinful) is to spend eternity where all weakness dwells (hell).

The only good thing I can honestly say about being weak is that God's strength is made perfect in our weakness, if we will surrender it to him. Having said that, I used to be ashamed of being born so weak (depressed), but now slowly but surely I am learning to glory in it, like Paul did. The other thing about my choice of words is that if I may be so bold as to say that God in these latter times is reaching out to America with all His might. For times they are a changin'. Now people live lies instead of the truth. More and more are moving backwards instead of forward in life. They embrace darkness instead of light, and to me it all stems from the worst one of all, they embrace and celebrate weakness for strength. That is why I believe the Spirit of God led me to frame my arguments that way as to draw a line through thoughts, feelings, words and deeds of an individual, a culture, a religion, a race, a political party, and the entire world.

There are a lot of people in darkness that are looking for the way so they can find the truth that they may obtain the life. If you take a quick look at segments of our culture, people are making big money by bragging about being weak-minded. This in turn leads millions and millions of children to be weak-minded as well, i.e., lust, hate, greed, pride, selfishness, violence, apathy, laziness, vengeance, disrespect, fear, self pity, and unforgiving. In effect they are teaching (programming) them to hate God, themselves, and their fellow man; in essence to hate life itself.

For anyone who thinks he knows the heart of God, knows that His heart is broken over the tremendous needless loss of life in this country. My mission impossible is to put a stop to it or die trying. Okay, just help as many as possible find the door to the cage. The truth about lies is that the weakness they produce will catch up with you sooner or later. One way or another they will find you out, and they will hurt you for a season, a lifetime or an eternity.

The all time weakest sight in the kingdom of darkness is a spiritual candy cane that is a person who is wrapped in pride and self pity. Deep inside they know their life is "kicked to the curb," and yet they are too proud to trust Jesus, so they just keep on taking a lickin'. The person in the kingdom of "light" is more like a push-pop. They know when to stand up for the truth and they know when to humble themselves to the truth. Instead of a lickin', they take a blessin'.

# TRUTH OR CONSEQUENCES

It has just now occurred to me that all the other spiritual self-help books I ever read told personal stories about the author's interaction with people to make his point clear. I just realized I don't have any interactions with people...just life. I think that is because this ain't about me, it's about us and the life we share. Anyway, next topic. Do you think it is wiser as opposed to not being wise to let the student instruct the teacher, or the criminal handle the police, or the child discipline the parent? Or how about the weak leading the strong, or maybe the emotional guiding the intellectual? As simple as it may sound, that is the exact case which is playing out in our nation—February 20, 2006. In my estimation we have a passive man (Reps) versus an angry woman (Dems). <u>Remember:</u> All of the subjects and topics covered in this book are spiritual. They may or may not be happening or exist, depending on whether you believe the truth or the lie.

Question: What kind of life would you have as an individual regardless of anyone else, if you only did what you felt like doing 100% - 90% - 80% of the time? What if you did not feel like holding down a job or feel like taking care of your responsibilities? Or how about if you felt like committing a crime of passion or violence, such as rape or molestation of an innocent child, or armed robbery for that matter, because you felt like you had to get your hands on some loot? What kind of life would you have or what if you just felt like doing nothing with your life, it's yours after all. What if 5, 10, 50, 100, 1,000, 1,000,000 or 20,000,000 people felt like you? What kind of country would this be?

What if you had a nation of 20,000,000 to 30,000,000 all colors, backgrounds, etc. whining and complaining about everything that did not go their way because they felt like they were being mistreated or victimized? This sounds to me like a society that is unstable, unraveling and highly implosive, sort of like when you have a screw loose or when you try and remove a nut from a bolt. What do they always tell you Lefty Lucy and Righty Tighty? All I can say is 100 gazillion nuts and loose screws can't be wrong. Now on the other hand, a person of intellect who not only is aware of his feelings, yet he uses his brain first to reach an intelligent decision regarding the issues of life. He needs to go to school to get an education so he will increase his or her chances of finding a job. He knows he has to keep a job to eat and take care of his responsibilities. The man of intellect has ups and downs and setbacks like anyone else, but he thinks before he acts so no matter what he feels like, he would never do to someone that which he would not want them to do to him or his loved ones. You tell me of the two types of people, which do you think would lead overall to a positive, progressive, and explosive nation full of hard work, peace, prosperity, and righteousness? As opposed to the negative, regressive, and implosive; a nation full of laziness, violence, poverty and unrighteousness (Leftist).

Now the plot thickens. What will happen when the two parties collide? Who will win, and who will lose? Strong versus weak, intellect versus emotion? The one thinks for himself, so he is independent and free to make the most out of his life for himself and his family which, by the way, he thinks life is the best thing since sliced bread. Is that where the term "a slice of life" comes from, I wonder. Anyway, the other guy never cared enough about himself to think what his life would be like if he only did what he felt like dong.

The people on the Left's power lies in lies. They gain control by using underhanded tactics of weakness, namely they cry and moan about how they need help. But because they never cared about life anyway, they just need help to help keep them feeling needy. It's an addiction. The political leaders on the Left use these poor needy people to gain leverage against the Right. For their ultimate goal of course is to have all Americans poor and needy, except for them and their families and friends. Of course, they would never admit it, but they are liars. They take after their father. The poor people on the Left have been lied to and so badly beaten spiritually that you could not open their eyes to the truth with a crow bar. I know, because I used to be one of them. No matter how they see themselves they act as needy children. Victims who need to be cared for. They can't see that they are the makers of their own destiny and environment and that they, as well as life, are full of potential to either implode or explode based on whether they believe the truth or lies. Life is what you make it, for the most part. You will reap what you sow; to the spirit is life (think), to the flesh is death (feel).

Now the party on the Right has a delicate dilemma on its hands. On the one hand you feel the pain and suffering of people in poverty. On the other hand, if you keep giving to those who are poverty stricken the means to stay poverty stricken, by giving them an endless stream of cash, to the tune of 6.5 trillion dollars, you do them a major disservice to the point where you show them extreme contempt and loathing. You suggest that they are not smart enough or strong enough to manage their own lives. Yet the leaders on the Left thrive on this situation, so they go around pretending that they are on the side of the little guy just to incur pity (weakness) to use as leverage. Since there are no little Americans, just little U.S. citizens, the only thing the Right can do is hold the line because giving in to weakness would be the death of us all. We must educate as many U.S. citizens as possible to become Americans; to feel the joy, freedom, and power of being in control of their own destiny.

# THE BLAME GAME

The Libs love to play the blame game almost as much as another fellow who is known as the accuser of the brethren. They seem to have a special interest in using it with my race, perhaps due to slavery there is a path of pity worn in our souls or that my race is so emotional we put emotion into just about everything we do. This is not necessarily a bad thing as long as it is kept under control by thinking. Side note: the devil's number one strategy of attack is to make you feel something, i.e. lust, hate, pride, self pity, laziness, jealousy, greed or vengeance. Can you imagine all the people who are dead or in jail or on the run because of out of control emotions?

Since 90% of Blacks vote Democratic, that would make just about every Black man and woman in jail now a victim of Liberalism. This is a tough pill to swallow, but the facts don't lie, and at this point in time I would like to set the facts straight about modern day slavery. The Acorn effect: what would happen if you were to plant an acorn (a seed)? Sooner or later you would grow an oak tree with all its different parts. You would have the roots, the trunk, the branches, the limbs, the leaves, the bark, the wood and last but not least, the acorns. The Libs used the same principle when they planted the seed of slavery in our culture through welfare and entitlement programs. They bought our loyalty, freedom, and dignity. Tell me, have you ever gone somewhere and paid for something and left it there or not used it for something? Of course not! Like the acorn, once the seed of slavery was planted, all they had to do is sit back and watch it grow all of the components of a plantation right before your eyes. You have slave masters, house Negroes, Aunt Jemimas, Uncle Toms, crops/field Negroes, plantations and slave traders. If you support the Liberal Democratic Party, then you are on the plantation. Black Americans need to wake up and "peep real game."

I will go one step further by going back to our ancestors who were brought here by force, and who suffered tremendous and brutal hardships filled with pain, misery, degradation, bondage, and death. They really had it <u>hard.</u> They were forced into it. We volunteered. They could not leave when they wanted to, even though it is hard to see we can still come and go as we choose. They were incredibly strong for what they endured, always hoping for a brighter day so that their descendants (us) might have a chance to be free. We, on the other hand, are incredibly weak; for what sane man would chain himself to death for the love of money? Even though we were snookered, we were Republicans when Lincoln freed our ancestors. I think it is high time to return to our spiritual, cultural, and political roots. Can you dig it!!

As much as it pains me to have to say this, our ancestors would be turning over in their graves if they saw how we are squandering this golden opportunity to live like decent civilized men and women. Being educated and raising our families to know God. To be able to enjoy all the many benefits this country has to offer. Things to do, see, and learn. We dishonor their sacrifice, legacy, blood and our very own future. To almost the entire hip-hop nation, you are the first batch of almost pure zeroes. You have created an entire lifestyle (which is really a death style) on being weak-minded. Just because you can pick up a gun or make a baby does not make you a man. I know you think you have a lot of heart because you are not afraid to die in these streets—but that's the whole problem, all heart and no brains. Why should you give your life away over some drugs or money? Your self worth and esteem is lacking greatly.

The unemployment rate among our people is 10.5% to 11%, double the national average. Why? Because this will breed an atmosphere for violence which is part of the recipe for destruction and continued enslavement of you, your kids, their kids and so on. You are digging a spiritual hole for our race, and by necessity some force will come along and cover you up. New Orleans was just a small example of depending on man instead of God. You feel me? Treat life like a joke and a game, then you and life will be one and the same. Treat life with respect and love, then your only limits are the stars above us.

News flash! This just in to all the rest of the Black Americans looking for someone to blame for slavery. Don't waste time blaming the White guy, blame God. It was He that allowed our ancestors to be brought over here so we would take part in His little taste of Heaven experiment where people from all walks of life could be free to go as far as your determination would take you. No matter, rich or poor, black, white, brown, yellow, male, female, young or old, to make the best of what you have and do your best to make it better for your offspring. Therefore, in my opinion, either learn how to forgive (especially since we were not around during slavery) or go back to Africa. In all seriousness, our distant relatives over there need our help big time. But how can we help them when we can't help ourselves? Okay. When will the spirit of the mighty men of valor return? Soon, I hope and pray.

The past is dead, the future holds promise. Like the hands of a clock on the wall, let us move to the right, go forward and make progress. Let us stop moving and looking backwards to the Left in time. Let the strong teach the weak wherever they may be.

The self-proclaimed leaders of the hip-hop nation should stop and take a long serious look at the devastation that their promotion of a weak, backward death style is causing, and that what they are promoting for their masters is killing our race. If you continue to promote the implosion, our future children will continue to grow weaker and weaker, and more and more angry and violent. If the Lord does not return or you do not repent, our children will be so unstable and weak they will hate everything in life that God put here to enjoy. The only thing that they will love is death and weakness, which will lead them to hell, so I ask you do you care for your own? The goal of life is not to prove how much you don't care and hate life, but to show how much you love it. It is the only one you will get. The truth can cut like a knife, hurt like the devil, yet heal like Heaven. If you look around the world you can see people in advanced stages of implosion after centuries of oppression. They have become so sensitive and emotional that they would rather die and kill other innocent people to believe that they have been wronged. I have observed this condition in all different capacities from political, racial, cultural, religious, economical and national. They all stem from the same source, weakness that is manifested by the lack of the truth.

## THE TRUTH

Where would we be without it? From math, science, chemistry, medicine, physics to engineering, astro and aerospace to modern technology to healthy and proper human behavior. All have their foundation and are maintained by the power of the truth. We as human beings, especially, are super highly advanced in the way in which our spirits, bodies, minds and souls operate, either in harmony with the truth or disharmony without it. We here in America owe all we have and enjoy to the unchangeable, immutable power of the truth. His name is Jesus!

# BOTTOM OF THE BARREL

What is at the bottom of the barrel anyway? It has been a longstanding belief that everything bad dwells at the bottom, all of the unwanted dregs of society. Yet I am referring to the bottom of the barrel in regard to what it is that has and is causing so many people to implode, and also the people who capitalize on other people's weakness and sorrow. Those that profit off misery are actually in the same boat as the victim. Their time of suffering just comes later. Is the answer in family upbringing, cultural environment or in government policies? I think these all play an important role in shaping and developing a person's outlook on life, and how he looks at himself. It is the latter of the two that play a bigger role than the former as to what a person will do with their lives.

Based on everything I have seen, heard, and learned of myself and people all over the world via the media, I think we are suffering from a perpetual spiritual inferiority complex that's being agitated and enforced by forces and powers of darkness and weakness. These forces continually pull and drive us to speak, think, feel, and act in ways that are totally contrary to our own well being and that of our fellow man as well.

In the book of Genesis, the Bible speaks of the fall of man in the Garden of Eden when he disobeyed God (his spiritual Father), and learned of the knowledge of good and evil (weakness and strength). Since the spirit of man is created in the image of God and having rebelled against God, man has been falling ever since within himself in spite of all the technological advances in medicine, science, and engineering. The heart of man still remains deceitful and desperately wicked. This is the reason for the condition of the world today, man going in one direction (down), and God going in another (up).

All of the hate, murder, pride, jealousy, greed, selfishness, lust, anger, and fear (sin) all came about because of man's disobedience to the truth that God knows best. God, being who He is, had to make a way to reconcile us to Himself without compromising His laws and integrity. His plan was to send the truth into the world to reveal the way that men could see the life again. That was the work Jesus completed on the cross, He defeated the kingdom of weakness and darkness there by giving all who really trust in Him the power to overcome sin (weakness, disobedience). The only problem is that man has been accustomed to being weak for so long, it is now ingrained in our physical beings and is expressed in this physical world. We have come to accept it as normal. Couple that with evil forces trying to keep us from realizing all the love, peace, joy and happiness that God had intended for our lives. We only see a small fraction of our potential spiritually, physically, emotionally and intellectually.

If you want to stop your life from imploding with weakness, selfishness and fear, then trust Jesus. Depending on your spiritual genetics, upbringing and environment as well as when you started your journey, and how much damage you have done to yourself, will make your story unique to you. Don't worry about anyone else but yourself.

Just what is a spiritual inferiority complex anyway? A S.I.C. is a group of negative, weak, destructive thoughts and feelings that lead to weak words and actions dealing with issues of low self esteem (self respect), no or low self confidence and no or low self worth. This in turn will always cause a person to do something to steal, kill and/or destroy their life, potential, and/or time, of not only them but anyone who gets too close to them, i.e. religious, cultural movements, races, and nations. All can implode.

There are different reasons for different types of implosions, individually or collectively similar to the three components of fire (fuel, spark, oxygen). A complex of weakness has usually three elements that start the vortex of implosion depending on whether it's a type "A" aggressive or type "B" passive personality. The type "A" person will usually attack other people because of their own sense of failure, and type "B" people will usually attack themselves. One expresses itself outward, the other inward. Both stem from the same source of weakness.

The combinations of the different reasons to implode are endless, and yet very predictable. The basic overall formula goes something like this. Type A or B personalities divided by low or no self esteem, self respect, self confidence (one or all three) multiplied by all of the lies they have ingested, whether by upbringing, culture, spirit or a person, plus all of the opportunities that life will present based on how they think and feel about themselves to express themselves. Even though everyone has their own unique story to tell, here are some basic examples: Type A male with no self confidence, respect or esteem, believes lies that he can't make it. Someone is holding him down, that's just the way it is. He feels trapped, turns violent, gets a gun, winds up dead or in jail. A Type B woman has low self esteem, low respect, believes lies that there is nothing special about her. That she deserves to be mistreated; she ought to be glad for what she can get. She usually ends up alone, a door mat, physically and mentally abused, out on a street corner on drugs and alcohol, suicidal, or becomes homosexual looking for love in all the wrong places.

A Type A woman with no or low self respect or esteem believes the lies that men and women are the same, that women are just as good or better than men (as if comparing apples to oranges would prove anything). They usually make a life of using their bodies and charm to break, crush, and use as many men as possible (if they are attractive). If not, they go gay with extreme anger towards men, the former lady may go there as well or she might just settle down with a wimpy whipping post for security's sake, and have a secret life on the side—wink, wink.

A Type B male with low or no self confidence or esteem also believes lies, especially those who have had no support from a man in his upbringing or an abusive role model, that he starts comparing himself to other images of what it means to be a man. Jesus is the pattern. He doesn't believe he measures up (so to speak). He sees and hears other men expressing their weakness so he assumes he must be gay.

Side Note: If you are a guy struggling with that form of weakness, 1) stop sleeping with all the women you can get your hands on, trying to overcompensate will only make you disrespect yourself even more. This will only make you weaker. Stop believing lies. God did not make you that way, and if He did, it's only to prove that He has the power to bring you out so you can help others. Also, stop comparing yourself to other men. Jesus is the only man whose approval you will need in this life.

F.Y.I. There is such a thing as spiritual genetics. God says in the Ten Commandments that He would visit the sins (weaknesses) down to the third and fourth generation of those who hate Him. That means that this fact is an incalculable variable which means no matter the type—the truth, lies or opportunities in your life— you may have to deal with one or more issues that are not your fault, but will be your responsibility. This is the price that must be paid for living in a fallen world. Two wrongs will not make one right.

F.Y.I. "Be all you can be in the Army." That was the slogan for the Army back in the '90s. You may not realize it, but that is the number one slogan in the spiritual realm as well. In other words, spirits want to manifest themselves in your life to the utmost of their and your ability. Example, the spirit of hate wants to consume you, and either convert or affect as many people as possible. The same goes for pride, jealousy, fear, greed, unforgiveness, anger, selfishness, ingratitude or lust (meet the armies of darkness, weakness and death).

Pop Quiz—Hypothetical: Suppose you went to the doctor for a checkup and he told you that you need to lose weight, stop smoking, eat right, get exercise, and get more sleep. And, by the way, you have cancer, but fortunately we caught it in time. We can have it out in no time flat. Would you say, "Yes doctor, please hurry up and remove it," or would you say, "Ah doc, you know cancer has a right to live too. It just wants to be all it can be." The doctor says, "But it will kill you eventually." You say, "Well at least the cancer will be happy."

The reason I'm spending extra time on this subject is because of the emasculation and feminization of men in America by the feminist movement. Our nation will see a pretty big shift to the

Left of the male role model image in America. Granted the spirit of lust does not care whether sexual immorality occurs between a man and a woman or two men and two women, except the former is easier to correct than the latter since Leftists always accuse others of the things they themselves are guilty of. We are not homo-phobes for wanting to live and raise our families in a normal environment. Those of you who are of that ilk are actually the hetero-phobes. You fear us and you feel uncomfortable because you are out numbered, so the only way for you to feel good is to have a majority rule. Even though you don't think it, that spirit will not stop ever. The more rights you get, the more it will want. It has happened in other civilizations throughout history. I am not trying to hurt anyone's feelings or make any one emotionally distraught, but what kind of America do you want? Land of the free, home of the brave, or land of the fiends, home of the gays? Jesus said, if anything causes you to sin (be weak), pluck it out or cut it off. It would be better to make it to Heaven blind or crippled than to have your whole body be cast into hell.

# GETTING TO KNOW YOUR ENEMY

A wise person once said, "Keep your friends close and your enemies closer." I would prefer this strategy in the figurative sense as opposed to a literal situation. I personally cannot stand a fake imposter crook who is an enemy, but pretends to be your friend; a being that presents themselves as an angel of light, and is really a devil.

Speak of the devil, here are a few observations on how your number one enemy operates against you and your family. Satan's power is in his craftiness/intelligence of the spiritual realm. His strength is in our weakness and our lack of knowledge of the spiritual realm.

The only way the devil can make you hurt yourself is if you have weakness in you, i.e. fear, pride, lust, to name a few. The more weakness you crucify, the less he can attack you, at which point he will try to make others attack you, family, friends, co-workers, etc. That's when you begin to realize that "greater is He that is in you than he that is in the world." This is why it is so important to know who you really are in Christ, because old things have passed away and all things have become new. You are a new creation in Christ so you have to let all of your old ways of thinking and feeling about yourself and others in life go. You have to see things from God's point of view. That is when you will have the power to overcome every situation you may go through, and you will see all things really do work together for good for those that love God, who are called according to His purpose (not yours).

The devil's number one spiritual weapon is fear. Fear is also the leading cause of heart disease in America. People die from a weak heart. Some people fear success, some fear failure, others fear rejection. Some fear loneliness or being alone, some fear adversity, strangers, death, life, the past, the future, change, love, the truth, God, the devil. Some fear taking a stand for what they believe. Fear of reaching out to help people in need. Fear of being normal. Fear of losing one's mind. Fear of pain. If we in America could just stop being afraid of our own shadows so to speak, we would live longer and have a much better quality of life.

People that fear standing up for the truth will invariably have the weakness to bend over for lies. Satan's number one double agent ally is the lukewarm Christian. A believer that is neither cold nor hot, but right in the middle, provides the perfect gray camouflage to weaken God's power and to advance his kingdom. The reason for so many lukewarm Christians is because of men and women who were not called to preach or pastor. Therefore, they have no idea what they are talking about. Also some did not wait for their time to come before they were ready to start a ministry. When God has prepared you for a ministry, it will all come together naturally. You will know how to make the Bible come alive; how to live the word and not just read the word. And most important of all, a good shepherd will lay down his life for his sheep. Some people like me are hard-headed and stubborn. God had to work on me a long time just to get me to this point.

How ironic it is that thugs, gangsters and hustlers willingly lay down their lives for their father (Satan) all for a few dollars and some drugs and sex. Additionally, there is a one-way ticket to hell. Yet God's children have more and better promises, including Heaven, but we cling to this life as if it was our home. No wonder the younger generation is attracted to the razor's edge; real is real, even if it's based in lies and weakness.

The thing that the thugs need to realize is that you cannot make people respect you at gun point. When you respect yourself, then they will respect you as well. Other than that, they'll just stand back and watch you kill yourselves and each other. There are a lot of good people on the Right who would like to put an end to this ridiculous situation. But in order to get real help, you have to want it. Life is not going to show you anything you are not trying to find. The only way someone can keep you down is if you agree to stay down, because as far as I know, cream always rises to the top.

The thing about Libs is they try their best to make people feel so ashamed about being poor. Last time I checked, there was no law against being broke. If there were, I would be in jail now. Being poor is not a crime, actually it is a golden opportunity to walk very close to God. Because you learn to depend on Him for everything, which will cause you to be rich in faith, and give you a more meaningful productive life than some people with tons of money who are too greedy and selfish to share, but it is a free country.

The largest and most dangerous mission field for America: just look at the Left. The saying that you can't see the forest for the trees is definitely true. When I was on the Left, I could not see how weak and backwards and unstable we all were, but now that I have escaped the madness it is as clear as day that the Liberal movement is for people that are weak, dumb, overly emotional, and who hate God. The silence of the lambs of God in America is deafening, and that's bad!! The conservative Christian right has done an outstanding job of holding this country together and should be commended by way of the ballot box. They have let their voice be heard, yet unfortunately when it comes to dealing with the Left, they seem to be afraid of a confrontation about who is right and who is wrong. The showdown is inevitable, in my opinion. The sooner the better, so that more lives may be saved. Not to mention weakness will drain the life out of you.

A little leaven will leaven the whole lump. Weak is as weak does. God wants you to embrace life with a positive attitude. The other fellow wants you to fear it. Strong is as strong does.

# WHERE HAVE ALL THE MIRACLES GONE?

The nature of the beast in America is overindulgence. We have so much to be thankful for in this country that we forget the rest of the world is not on our level. We forget to be thankful for all of our blessings, which will cause us to develop an attitude of ingratitude, as if we were entitled to the best of everything.

This weakness has invaded the church. Believers think that God is here to only meet their material needs, which is pure weakness. Our job is to preach the gospel first. Seek ye first the kingdom of God and His righteousness, and all these things shall be added unto you. The reason there are so few real miracles in the church is because the weakness of the world is in the church via the lukewarm pastors who are content to get paid and not preach the word of God for fear of losing money from their flocks. (His fleece.)

One thing you have to understand about the Bible, the authors were talking to different people at different stages of maturity, themselves included. It is theologically and practically dangerous to claim things that you don't have the faith, knowledge or understanding of certain laws that apply to your situation. This includes anything from health, money, family, career, etc. People have a tendency to get angry and disillusioned with God if He does not do what they want. A lot of people will walk away and some will follow in rebellion (lukewarm). They constantly grieve the Holy Spirit, thinking that God's job is to make them happy according to what they want, i.e. money, houses, cars, a mate, etc.

That is the way I used to be, so I know it when I see it in others. It does take one to know one. God's job is to conform you to the image of His Son. He will use whatever means are at His disposal to accomplish this goal. He wants to make you whole or positive in your thoughts, feelings, words and actions.

In my humble opinion, this issue of the lukewarm person is the main problem of the church in America. The lukewarm person basically stands in the door of the church, half inside and half outside. He won't let the light of the truth get out and he won't let anyone get in. These are people who find they are still going to clubs, drinking, smoking, using profanity, having sex with people they are not married to, gossiping, etc. The person trying to find God thinks that this is normal and begins to copy the same behavior, which causes a sea of gray uselessness, neither hot nor cold. The Lord said His name was blasphemed among unbelievers because of us. He also said that He would spit lukewarm people out of His mouth. He also said that they were wretched, miserable, poor, blind, and naked. For the Lord to make such harsh statements like that, the lukewarmers must really tick Him off. He mentioned that people in the middle of the road should purchase gold from Him refined in fire.

Back when I was young, I took to heart what the Lord had said. Be hot or cold. Since I could not stay hot for very long I made the most dangerous and destructive decision in my life. I decided to be cold. I literally stopped trying to follow the Lord. I spent the next 20 years wandering in the badlands, the muck and mire, the wilderness where I learned the meaning of being "sifted like wheat." I believe that's what happens to a person whose implosion is so great that an individual will watch his hopes, dreams, potential, career, friends, family, resources, health, peace (sanity), and "will to live," all go up in smoke.

That was the foolish path I chose, and for some 20 years I spent time in the oven of life "doing my thing," spinning my wheels (in the mud), trying to find meaning and purpose in life, which without the truth of life is impossible. Clue: to get the most out of life is to make a positive direct contribution to life, i.e. thoughts, words, feelings, and actions.

The prodigal son and the backslider (assuming they make it back to the father's house) can share a tremendous amount of wisdom from their experience, if they are willing to purchase that gold from the Lord that has been refined in the fire. That fire is of obedience. Obedience is the fire that purges us from our sins (weakness). This fire burns the flesh by not allowing it to have control over your life. So when it is time to pray or read the Bible or testify of the Lord, you will be able to accomplish it. The more gold you purchase (obey), the richer you will become (spiritually). Just as we as human beings really enjoy the feeling of taking a shower or bath and putting on a brand new set of clothes, the whole nine; socks, shoes, underwear, pants, hat, shirt, jacket, watch, bracelet, ring(s), chain(s), plus the hairdo, etc. I am told that's a really good feeling.

This is the same type of desire that the Lord has for you to desire for yourself from Him. He wants your spiritual clothes to be top shelf, name brand, instead of being clothed spiritually in pride, lust, lies, envy, greed, and unforgiveness. He would much rather see us clothed in humility, purity, truth, generosity, patience, and confidence.

# BORN AGAIN, NOT STILLBORN

The one good thing about knowing the Lord or becoming cold (spiritually dead) again, you can clearly see both sides of the coin. You can see good and evil, hot versus cold, right versus wrong, strong versus weak. After having the knowledge of good and evil, it is clear that any sane person would choose life versus death, spiritually, physically, intellectually, and emotionally, which transfers to your thoughts, words, feelings and actions. This will form your habits, which will form your character, which will form your destiny.

In the Bible, the Lord talks about being born again. He said you must be born again in order to enter the kingdom of God (Heaven), John 3:3. Since everything emanates from the spiritual realm, it stands to reason that like a physical baby being born fully formed with hands, feet, brain, heart, eyes, nose, etc, even if the child is normal in every way, except spiritually, there is no life in the child; sad but true.

Likewise being born again is a formative process in which a potential believer goes through what includes the forming of his spiritual body, mind, hands, feet, etc. As the Holy Spirit brought Jesus to term and delivered Him alive into this realm, we must be brought to term and born alive into the spiritual realm.

As far as I can tell, a lot of Christians believe that being sealed by the Holy Spirit is the same as being filled by the Holy Spirit. When you accept Jesus as Lord and Savior, this is the authorization for the Spirit to begin work in your life to conform you to the image of the Lord that you hopefully one day will be born alive into the kingdom of God. The only way to ensure that this occurs is to be crucified, not cruci-tried or cruci-lied. You have to put your flesh to death in order to be born alive into God's kingdom. Even though we will never have complete 100% victory over the flesh in this life, there are ways to determine how far we have to go to reach our goal to be born again. The Holy Spirit gains controlling interest of your being when He does not have to continually fight with you over obvious sins, i.e. sex, drugs, violence, and external sins, which are indeed grieving to Him; then He starts on the internal ones: pride, envy, hate, deceit, etc.

You will reach a point where you look at your world and see how your actions (smoking, lying, partying, lusting, violence, etc.) either add to the problem of sin, or solve the problem. That's why some people are cruci-lied. They practice deception as a way of life. Some people have cruci-tried. They started but just gave up. The road that leads to eternal life is hard to find, and hard to follow.

What would have happened if Jesus would not have stayed on the cross but kept coming down? We would still be in our sins. The same thing applies to you. If you keep coming down off of your cross, you prohibit yourself from being born again. A lot of people measure out their sins over a period of time until they are in their 50's, 60's and 70's. I have seen people who have known of the Lord for 30 - 40 years, and they are the same as they were when they first met Him (stillborn). The same applies to a lot of churches. If there is life in a church, there will be growth in numbers, but that does not mean the fake church of Satan where people seek to use God to get rich or find a mate or some such carnal thing. "Seek ye first the kingdom of God and all these things shall be added unto you."

The Bible says that those that hunger and thirst after righteousness will be filled (Matthew 5:6). That means you must be emptied of self first before you can be filled. I spent 20 years being emptied of self and learning the truth based on living lies. Until you overcome pride, self righteousness and arrogance, you will never see the kingdom of Heaven.

The immaculate lover, God, will not continue to give Himself to someone who is unfaithful. He will not cast His pearls before swine. Those that come to God must believe that He is God, and that He rewards those who diligently seek Him.

The Holy Spirit is in the process of drilling to the core (center) of your being. Once he gets there, and after battling against all of your weaknesses, pride, self pity, and consortium, eternal life will start to quicken your life. Then your ministry will fall into place. The Lord will speak to you in your situation, or through people or nature, but you will know it is Him.

Three ways to know that eternal life is starting to flow in you:

1. Your concern for the lost will grow. The more the growth, the more the life.

2. The Holy Spirit will not have to fight with you to stop sinning (being weak). You will become tired of being tired of yourself.

3. Rivers of living water will flow from the well within you. The deeper the well, the sweeter the water of joy, love, and peace, that will grow. People will want to be around you because you have eternal life in you.

You will, in effect, become fishers of men. Jesus said, if He be lifted up, He would draw all men unto Himself.

Believers need to keep their eyes on the prize—to make it to Heaven, follow Jesus closely. That is why there are so few miracles in America. Overindulgence is the nature of the beast in America. We need to collectively get a hold of ourselves to stop the madness, or we risk staying caught in a loop until our life is wrecked by weakness.

# MY FELLOW AMERICANS

I am amazed at how those three words, one little phrase, could contain and embody so much power. That they could be so heavily laden in responsibility, expanding from border to border, from coast to coast, from moving forward in time to moving backwards in time, all the way to reaching the heights of Heaven to the pits of hell. Contained in those three words is so much love, so much hope, so much work, so much pride, so much peace, so much opportunity, so many hopes, so many dreams, so many victories, so many advances, so much knowledge, so much humility, so much goodness, so much joy, so much caring, so much strength, so much history, so many hardships, and struggles, so much freedom, and so much truth.

There are so many things to be thankful for in this country that I am in awe and very glad to be an American. Yet I would be remiss if I did not address the other side of the coin. Unfortunately, there is also so much hate, so much fear, so much lust, so much envy, so much selfishness, so much weakness, so much pessimism, so much misery, so much failure, so many lost hopes and dreams, so much ignorance, so many setbacks, so much apathy, so much arrogance, and so much evil.

These are the two sides of the coin that we as fellow Americans should either embrace wholeheartedly or reject outright. In my opinion, the golden rule should be applied, "Do unto others as you would have them do unto you." Yet it is becoming increasingly apparent that a considerable number of Americans not only don't care about themselves, but also do not care for their fellow Americans.

If America is going to grow and thrive, we will eventually have to find a way to address and deal with this problem for all of our sakes, and our children's future.

The bottom lines is, are you part of the head or are you part of the tail? Are you part of the solution or the problem? This is regardless of your color, black, white, brown, red and yellow, whether male or female, young or old, rich or poor, handsome or homely, powerful or powerless. As our troops lay down their lives to protect our freedoms, how can we not be willing to do any less if we really love this land of ours; the only home we have. As an American, I believe this nation is worth defending from enemies, both foreign and domestic.

My fellow Americans, where do you stand or where will you fall, on the side of the truth or of the lies? What we can or what we can't do, what we can or what we can't be—the future of our nation is in our hands.

# TID BITS

American culture versus multi-culture. If it ain't broke, don't fix it. People that come to this country should learn the language, respect the borders and laws, and embrace the real culture, which is honesty, independence, and hard work.

World breakdown. Nation by nation. If our nation is not so great, then why do so many people risk their lives to get here? People in America don't know what poverty and oppression from the government really is. Because of the Left, a lot of Americans have devolved into spoiled, immature, selfish brats, who instead of trying to grow up and act like an adult, would much rather bring the entire nation down to their level. This is the trademark of Leftists all over the world, Liberalism, Socialism, Communism, and radical Muslims, from China, Cuba, former U.S.S.R., North Korea, Venezuela, Iran, Mexico, France, Germany, Canada, and various nations in the Middle East, Africa and Europe.

The leaders of these nations seek to gain and maintain control over spiritually uneducated people by turning them into immoral, materialistic, sex addicts whose only concern is for self. The foundation for Liberalism is self righteousness. This is why America should promote democracy around the world. It would be better for people to learn to be free than to learn to be slaves.

Poor people with dignity and opportunity don't waste time playing the blame game. They usually don't stay poor forever either, sort of how cream always rises to the top.

Who would ever have thought that the armies of darkness were actually, at their core, armies of weakness fueled by self pity and fear?

Where are you in your life? Are you in control of yourself? Do you know where you are going? Do you know what spiritual road you are on?

A lot of people on the right are shocked and amazed at the movies from Hollywood that are anti American, and anti President Bush.

Also certain television programs, plus classrooms and universities, are anti war, anti democracy, anti Capitalism, anti traditional America, and anti God. They are all just acting up to compensate for all of the Democrats' smelly political defeats.

God usually fires a warning shot, unlike the vice president (jokingly) before he puts in work. He that has ears to hear, let him hear.

Mommas don't let your babies grow up to be couch potatoes or they may end up like me, spending an awful amount of time noting the similarities and differences between the Right and the Left, fact or fiction, reality and art, too much T.V., too many movies or was it? Take for example the rock and the hard place that the Dems and Reps have the American people trapped in (which by the way are the people I am committed to). On the Left they seek to turn the nation into immoral infants in grown people's bodies. They want to tax the working middle class, businesses and the rich out of existence, which by the way are the people who pay to keep the nation running. This will eventually cause the nation to implode like the Soviet Union did. The Reps seem to want to spend taxpayers' hard earned money, in this administration anyway. The Reps seem obsessed with making international business deals that leave some Americans wondering whose side they are on. The issue that sticks in my craw is the borders and illegal aliens. Why the President does not seem to care about the nation's internal stability is totally beyond me. Looking at Washington today appears to be a real life version of good cop, bad cop. Is the fix in?

The truth about the Right and the Left, the plain simple fact of the matter, is that one direction has at its core the truth, which it attracts and exudes, expressed in the form of independence, freedom, strength, progress, stability and success. The other direction at its core is lies, which it in turn attracts and exudes, manifested in the form of enslavement, weakness, regression, instability, and failure.

The line between the two sides runs through every man, woman, and child. It also runs through all of our society, culturally, politically, religiously, and last but not least, spiritually which by the way is where the other parts of society emanate. There are only two sides to spirituality—truth or lies. The issue becomes murky when people get confused as to which way is the truth, and what is the best way to proceed in life—which is to follow truth versus the lies that are wrong and overall destructive.

Even though there are people on both sides of the aisle that belong to the other, some on the Left belong on the Right, and some on the Right belong on the Left. However, in my observation, there are millions upon millions that are on the Left which would join the Right if they could see the truth, and there are some on the Right that belong on the Left: White supremacists, Aryan nation, K.K.K., R.I.N.O.S., any person, group or movement that believes in lies, hate, violence, oppression, suppression, either by force or psy-ops. They all belong on the Left. They are an implosion on humanity. The destabilizing, unraveling, imploding effect of Leftism can be seen all around us starting with their desire for the U.S. to pull out of Iraq, which by the way would please the heck out of our enemies. (The enemy of my enemy is my friend.) Culturally in the Black community, people with tons of God-given talent, gifts, and potential (and not just in sports) are afraid to do their best, and to be their best. Religious people who believe in murder and violence to obtain peace with their god and fellow man, not to mention religious people on the Left, are spiritually in bed with the world, even though the Bible says clearly not to love the world nor the things of the world (1 John 2:15). Those that cherish the world's point of view (Left) cannot have the love of the Father in them.

One of the most appalling attempts of Leftism is the attack on school children by way of introducing them to sexuality before their time. Also, they seek to dumb down the children with outcome-based education. The list goes on and on.

Then we all know of politicians on the Right who actually belong on the Left, i.e. Republican in Name Only = R.I.N.O.'s.

On a more internal personal note, good mental, physical, emotional, and spiritual health stems from a positive, optimistic attitude towards yourself and life. Do not become unstable until you spoil yourself rotten, no matter whether you are Black, White, rich or poor (yes, even poor people can spoil themselves), young or old, male or female. The last time I checked anything spoiled or rotten gets thrown in the trash. In this case that would be the ghetto, the bottom of the barrel, a place where Leftism can be seen clearly, a place of high stress, hopelessness, crime, violence, despair, and weakness, which usually leads to a lot of drugs, alcohol, mindless sex, and parties, not because they have something to celebrate, but to escape the misery and pain that is their reality.

I personally believe that poor people (of which I am one) with dignity can turn a ghetto into a place of beauty and a work of art. If only the people would think right-minded and see themselves and each other as being worthy of respect and honor (like human beings). Either way, something will have to be done to prevent the wave of destruction and despair that is coming. I think the local governments see the danger. In my neighborhood, for instance, there are billboards up all over my city that say, "Suicide is preventable." Do they know something they are not saying? Hmm.

The reason that Leftism seems so popular and acceptable to so many different factions, is because they are shape shifters. They will tell you whatever you want to hear, which basically means they are spineless, no backbone, no truth; any lie will do as long as you believe it and take it to heart. Leftism doesn't want to take away your rights; they actually want you to give them up willingly.

The Leftists are tolerant of any and everything, and anybody, except for the truth. They cannot change the truth so they seek to distort it, cover it up, or remove the truth altogether.

The Republicans in Washington appear to be doing almost everything in their power to aid the Dems in validating a culture of corruption, thereby giving the Libs the House and Senate in 2006 (good politician, bad politician.). Since we have enemies in the camp and at the gate, the conservative base will have to grow a pair and hold the line as if our lives depended on it because it may very well be that way...

# FINAL THOUGHT

For those of you who were like me in school, who didn't do too well with math and spelling, those of you who can't put 2 and 2 together, those that can't read the handwriting on the wall, allow me to do the math and spell it out for you. Anything or anyone who moves to the Left, either in a circular motion or in a linear direction, will destabilize, unravel, implode, revolve backwards and retract spiritually, emotionally, physically, intellectually, culturally, politically and religiously.

Every force in the spiritual and physical universe is against Leftism. From nature everything with life expands upward, outward, and forward—a blade of grass, a fruit tree, the birth of a life, reptile, mammal, human, the rotation of the earth, sun, solar system, universe, physical engineering, every nut and loose screw, time itself from the hands of the clock on the wall, and history. Leftism has failed time and time again. At present Leftism has all but ruined the Black community, and their future. The future has no hope for someone who is scared to face it. Having mental and physical health and a sound mind is the key to good health. God's kingdom is positive, but the Leftists have robbed Him of the joy of being with His creations, which is basically a case of spiritual rape as far as what they could have had compared to what they received from Leftism (a bill of goods). The only force to agree with you is the prince of weakness and his kingdom of darkness. A black hole of outer space is the only thing that symbolizes Leftism. I am actually a lefty (south paw) so if I can change, anyone can.

The only real hope for the Dems' core base is to move to the right of the Republicans (yeah, right!). If the Libs could get over their extreme case of self righteousness and fear of freedom, the Left could see that the Right is not comprised of fascist imperialists because we follow God, not man. Before the foundation of the world when job assignments were being handed out, the question was asked, "Who shall we send and who will go for us." And I said, 'Here am I Lord, send me." The rest will be history. The Lord would rather you all come to Him, but if not, then there is a remnant that He is interested in; a number only He knows. The

221

door remains open through His only son Jesus Christ, whereby you can receive forgiveness for all of your sins. His spiritual blood can cleanse you from all of your weakness. His word can heal your heart and mind. You can be made whole. It may not be easy, and it might be painful sometimes, but it's worth it. After all, look at the alternative. Choose "The Way," choose "The Truth," and choose "The Life."

Amen.

# TO BE (SAVED) OR NOT TO BE (SAVED)

That is the question, whether a person who is once saved is always saved or whether a person has an obligation of a changed, committed and righteous life to affirm and confirm that this is a believer's statement of faith. I believe this question has to be one if not the most important question to be answered on this side of eternity. For you see, some people are resting (trusting) in the truth, and some are resting in lies. There are people who are going to be in for a very rude awakening.

If you would be so kind as to allow this unlearned, unscholarly, scarcely educated layman, who has been both hot and cold for the Lord, try most humbly to put into proper context the correct attitude, direction and temperature of a person on fire for the Lord, based on the scriptures (New Testament), and my personal experience and gifts of wisdom and discernment.

This is a very large and difficult subject to cover. It is also very necessary because souls are hanging in the balance.

F.Y.I. Alert: I intentionally did not give every chapter and verse in this book because the Bible says to search the scriptures wherein ye think ye have salvation. If I were to tell you where every verse was, you would go directly to that verse and not read the rest of the chapter, nor perhaps understand the context in which it was written. The Bible says, "Those that come to God must believe that He is, and that He is a rewarder of those that diligently seek Him." The Bible also says that a sluggard will put his hand to the dish, and be too lazy to take it out. He also will cry out, "There's a lion in the street! A lion in the street," and will turn over on his couch. Those proverbs basically mean that a person who is too lazy to take care of himself or try to save himself, probably is not reading this book anyway. So believe me when I say, like a certain spaghetti sauce says, "It's in there." It really is.

At the heart of the matter, well, it really is the heart. The Lord said, "Out of the abundance of the heart the mouth speaks." He also says, "As a man thinketh in his heart, so is he." The Bible states that we should guard our hearts, for out of it come all the issues of life. The Bible also says that the heart is deceitful and desperately wicked, who can know (understand) it? And last but not least the Bible says that God tests (tries) the hearts of men to reveal what's in them and to direct them.

How can it be that whether you like it or not, or even acknowledge it or not, that the most pivotal point in all of human history is centered on one man. The man Jesus Christ. Even as we mark a certain point in history as either B.C. (before Christ) or A.D. (after His death). According to His testimony every man and woman on the face of the earth will have to deal with the issue of who you were B.C. and who you are A.D. Having heard His revelation of an eternal after life, a place with two eternal kingdoms, Heaven, a place of life, strength, love, truth, peace, and joy; and Hell, a place of death, weakness, hate, deceit, misery and sorrow.

Although some people have had a near death experience and a few have been revived from death, no one has had the power to bring themselves back from the other side for a do over. As I state the obvious, it still amazes me how we get so busy in our lives that some of us don't take time to really think about whether he is telling the truth. And if he is telling the truth, what should we do about it while we have the time? Eternity is an awful long time to suffer on account of being too busy to deal with the truth. And what about the rest of my fellow Americans who say they believe in a God? Statistics indicate almost three out of four, 70% to 75% of U.S. citizens make that claim. The Bible says that, "Even the demons believe and they tremble." Just to say you believe in God is nothing without there being a real eye opening experience in which you see the activities of the world as they really are, full of hate, lust, anger, envy, pride, greed, vengeance, etc. Which, by the way, according to the effect these qualities have on an individual and society, the whole world is all weakness and death spiritually, emotionally, intellectually and physically. So if you don't believe in Jesus, you will still have to deal with Him sooner or later. And if you say you believe, but are still living in sin willfully—lying, stealing, cheating, fornicating, adultery, drugs, drinking, smoking—then either you are not telling yourself the truth (denial) or you are trapped in your own weakness (sin). The Lord came to seek and save the lost and to call the sinners to repentance. According to what's at stake, the stakes could not be any higher—your eternal resting place or your eternal tormenting place. The world (humanity) is in a slow death spiral. Just because it looks good, sounds good, and feels good, does not mean that it's good for you.

The whole point of this topic is to determine what our proper mind set, attitude, and perspective should be, and to determine whether we really believe the truth (Jesus), see the world as it really is (dying), and do not want our own lives to be controlled by sin (weakness).

So here we go, the Lord said the path that leads to destruction is broad and wide, and there are many who find it. He also said, the path that leads to eternal life is straight and narrow, and only a few find it. The question remains with all of our hopes, dreams, desires, goals, plans and potential. What would it profit a man to gain the whole world and lose his soul?

The Bible says, "Let each man with fear and trembling seek out his salvation." It also says the race is not given to the swift or the strong, but the one that endures to the end. The Bible seems to imply that this is a life long race that we need to run carefully and vigilantly. The Bible also says the devil goes around as a roaring lion seeking whom he may devour (lions are known for attacking the weakest members in a herd). Even as most Americans are either overweight, out of shape or downright obese, so likewise is the churchgoer who takes in too much of the bread of life (the word) without exercising their faith which will lead you to become slow, weak and lazy. A sitting duck is always easier to hit than a moving one. When the hunted becomes the hunter, life takes on a whole new meaning. That's when you start to realize the tremendous power and authority of your words and actions in the kingdom of light. You will become fishers of men.

In establishing a proper mind set, attitude and perspective, we need to motivate ourselves to give it all we've got, to run the race and not look back until we each cross our own finish lines, to love the

Lord (run) with all of our hearts, minds, souls and strength, and to let go of everything in this world that would slow us down (besetting sins), not only for your own sake, but for your family and friends as well. The truth of the matter is that God wants to know how deep or how shallow your love is. This is His test of the heart that reveals who you are, what you are worth (based on your beliefs), and where you belong in eternity. The Lord said those that seek to save their lives (selfish, self righteousness) would lose it (die in your sin). Those that lose their life (humility, sacrifice, righteousness) would find it. The measure of a man is not in his possessions.

A salmon swimming upstream is about the best analogy I can think of. Not only do you have your own vulnerabilities that make bears want to eat you, you have a rushing rapid that's trying to keep you back. This is like the weight of the world on your shoulders. I guess that's what the Lord meant when He said you must deny yourself (daily), pick up your cross and follow Him.

Which brings me to my final point. In America, there are two mind sets, some people believe once saved, always saved, and the other group believes that salvation even though by grace through faith requires participation on our part in the crucifying of the flesh (self). God wants to see if you will view sin as He does, and want it out of your life as much as possible. "Those that hunger and thirst after righteousness will be filled (satisfied)." People who believe "once saved, always saved," take a complacent, lackadaisical approach to salvation in my opinion, a sort of "what will be will be" approach. They seem to take an "it's not my fault," attitude (responsibility) for their life. It's God's or somebody else's. I used to think like that when I was a Leftist. There are people whom I love that will not let go of their sin, and they think they will cut a special deal with God. They say God knows your heart. Yes, He does. He knows that it's deceitful and desperately wicked, and that you would use a pity party in a New York minute. The Bible says God is not mocked. Whatever a man sows that shall he reap, to the flesh, death, but to the Spirit, life. In the majority of the churches I attended on the Left, the pastors spend most of the time preaching on either healing the body because of the weak, implosive state of not taking responsibility for ourselves and neighborhoods, or to try and trick God into giving us money. Just as God will not give you more than you can bear, neither will He give you blessings you can't handle. The Bible says you have not because you ask not. You ask and don't receive because you want to use it for your own selfish desires. If poor people would love God more than the love of money, He would make people give you money. You would not have to chase money, money would chase you. Don't believe me, try it and see.

The Lord said, "Not every one that saith unto me, Lord, Lord, shall enter into the kingdom of heaven," but He would say to them, "I never knew you: depart from me, ye that work iniquity." There was a man also who made it to the actual wedding feast, but did not have a wedding garment, and he got tossed as well. The Lord said, "Many are called, but few are chosen." The Bible also says, if the righteous scarcely make it in, where will there be room for the ungodly and the unjust? Only God actually knows who is His. Yet if we strive with all of our might to realize how weak we are and let the grace of God through faith conform us into the image of Jesus, this is the way to Heaven.

There is a difference between a Leftist and Leftism. A Leftist is a willful person who knows exactly what they are doing in regard to their cultural, political, and religious endeavors. Leftism is the product (victims) of Leftists. They are the brainwashed victims who are reduced to angry violent people being manipulated by psy-ops in music, religion, or politics. They have given up control of their lives from God to a man. The utterly horrific thing about Leftists is that even though by their very spiritual nature they are weak, evil, dying and backwards, if they can get in front of a religion, a race, or a nation, they will destroy any and all who follow or do not oppose them.

These words may seem harsh, but what is worse, seeing people starve to death because of tyrants, seeing people brutally oppressed by wicked regimes, or not to mention seeing people brainwashed through politics and culture (Leftism) to believe that life has no meaning outside of material and immediate gratification? This is why God saved us by grace through faith. Your faith is the supernatural force that gives you the power to stand up and tell a dying world to repent. It is not about mere works, lest any man should boast.

Truth and lies are alike in one regard, they both resonate from here to eternity and back again. Light into light, darkness into darkness. That is why tails don't make good heads and heads don't make good tails. The trick is to know which is which. (You shall know a tree not by how it looks, but by the fruit it bears.)

My friend, God does know your heart. He knows that He left a place in it that only He can fill. Try as you might with all the pleasures and activities of this dying world, they will be in vain.

## ALTAR CALL

So to the Leftist and the victims of Leftism, if you are sick and tired of watching your one and only life implode in slow motion day by day, bit by bit; if you are tired of watching life pass you by; and if you are tired of all your God-given potential being sifted like wheat. If you are tired of being controlled by fear, anger, jealousy, hate, and lust; if you are tired of your soul being stretched to the four winds (thoughts to the south, feelings to the north, words to the east, actions to the west); and if you are tired of being trapped in the belly of the beast via violent crime. If you are tired of watching your family, race, neighborhood, city, state, country, and world, destabilize, unravel, and disconnect itself from reality. If you are tired of seeing (as a man) little children and women being raped, abused and killed. If you are tired of feeling helpless, hopeless and confused about the life we all share; tired of watching weakness overwhelm you and this world. If you are tired of going out of this world butt backwards, and tired of being lonely, afraid, and worried. If you have come to the point that the thing you once enjoyed so much has turned into an addiction, and now you are trapped and tired of overeating, gambling, drug buying and selling illegal and prescription drugs; tired of the sex/porno addiction, and tired of the cigarettes (cancer sticks). If you are tired of being tired with no real and lasting hope or joy in this life, then cry out to Jesus with all of your heart and He will show you the way, the truth, and the life—guaranteed.

# ON THE OTHER HAND (RIGHT)

My new found fellow conservative Republicans, both secular and Christian—greetings in the name of the Lord.

Would you have believed in a zillion years that the hope and future of the civilized world is now resting squarely on your shoulders?

The reason I can make such a bold, broad and sweeping statement is because politically, culturally and religiously, Leftism has infected the entire world to varying degrees. There are a few small pockets of Rightists throughout the world, but not of any real or immediate significance.

As I stated before, everything emanates from the spiritual realm, primarily the laws that have founded, blessed and promoted this nation to the pinnacle of civilized history. These laws which came from God have made America what she is today. In a few short years, some 230, she has continued to grow and evolve, giving aid and comfort to billions around the world. Yet as I said before, it was the establishment of God-given moral laws that made this nation possible. So if there is any consolation to be had from this you White guys on the Right, know this: it is not you the Leftists hate; it's God. They don't hate President Bush; it is because he believes in God. They believe mankind can govern itself without God's help, which is pure lunacy. They are playing right into Satan's hands and don't even know it. Some are blinded by lust, pride, greed, self pity, selfishness, hate, jealousy, unforgiveness, laziness, or power because they hate the truth of Jesus. They pull backwards into darkness. They foolishly think that if they grow their numbers into the billions, they will have enough power to override the truth. They may one day overpower us, just in sheer numbers if America does not wake up. Yet we are counted as sheep for the slaughter. But they will never ever be able to change the truth, not one trillionth.

If you secular conservatives would take your head out of the political sand and open your eyes, you would see that we have our hands full and our work cut out for us. I don't know about you guys, but I am not going out like a sniveling coward. Plus since you guys are already leaning to the right, you may as well go all the way to the cross, and know what it means to live.

If you secularists on the right wish to keep all of the toys, bells and whistles you have, I would strongly suggest you team up with the Christians to make the Republicans in Washington a few offers they can't refuse. For they have obviously been seduced with Leftism as per all of the over-the-top earmark spending, the pork barrel spending, and allowing certain nations to have access to our country's more sensitive infrastructure concerning national security.

Speaking of national security, what about the illegal alien crisis? I am greatly troubled that the President did not drop the ball on this one. He never even picked it up. He just kicked it. The politicians on the Left and the Right are playing a game of kick ball trying to see if America will lose interest and go back to being self absorbed. I don't know whether to laugh or cry when I hear people talk about glorified amnesty programs. What in the world makes them think that people who broke the law to get here will respect the law after that? If they don't respect your laws, then they don't respect you or this country.

The President keeps saying we are a nation of immigrants. That's not exactly true, as Native Americans were already here. Not to mention my race did not volunteer to come here of their own free will, unless you consider immigration via guns, chains, and slave ships viable. Outside of that, this is a nation of immigrants, legal ones, not illegal ones. The President also says they do the jobs that the Americans, who we pay to sit on their butts, won't do.

Do you mean to tell me there are twelve million jobs that Americans won't do? Since I don't own a television (thank God), I did not see the protestors in L.A. There were 500,000 people demanding the right to break the law. There is something ominously ironic about that.

I think for the eye of the storm and the rest of the Libs who can't get the big picture, try looking at a little one, i.e. what if you had a house and a family and all of a sudden people just started coming over uninvited, eating your food, drinking your water, using up all your resources that you worked hard to provide for your family? How would you feel? What would you do?

The thing I can't help but wonder is what if a half million Mexicans had the actual courage to stand up and tell their President, like they told ours, that they demand their rights? Would there be rejoicing or mourning in Mexico? Would freedom ring or would shots ring out? Has this nation become so feminine that she will bend over so easily? Will she spend the rest of her days being strong-armed and bullied by cultural, political, and religious Leftists? Do nice guys and gals always finish last? If so, what will they leave for their children? United we stand: black, white, brown, yellow, American culture; but divided we fall: African American, Hispanic American, Asian American, European American—Multi-culturalism.

To the believers in America, now would be a good time to wake up completely and get ready for what is to come. The stage is set. All the props are in place. The lights are on, and the orchestra is cued. The cameras are rolling, and the actors are in place. Quiet on the set! Quiet on the set! To live by His word or to die by His word in America. Scene I, Take I—Lights, Camera and Action!!!

The Director

## TO THE BRETHREN OF THE CHRISTIAN CONSERVATIVE RIGHT:

We, few who are surrounded by the deep dark blue sea of the Left, greet you; as it were with a healthy hearty right hand of fellowship in the name of our Lord and Savior Jesus Christ.

Gentlemen of the faith, these are indeed perilous times in which we live. The stakes are tremendously high. The effects of political, cultural, and religious Leftism are wreaking havoc on our nation and the world. Leftism (backwardness) will eventually destabilize civilization as we know it.

It appears to me that we have been hand picked by our heavenly father for such a time as this before the foundation of the world, to set the stage for what must soon come to pass.

Since we don't actually know when our Lord will return, we must dig in and hold the line to the best our ability. This is indeed a glorious opportunity the Lord has bestowed on us—to purchase pure gold tried in the fire. The fire for where sin abounds grace does much more abound.

In light of the aforementioned information we believe the Holy Spirit is leading us to start a new movement of men moving in one spirit and one accord, in order to bring glory to our God and King. To accomplish this mission we must unite, organize and mobilize the body of Christ in a forward and positive direction (Heavenward). We believe that in Christ all men are brothers no matter their color or nationality. We believe that two men cannot walk together unless they agree on a direction, i.e. forward vs. backward (right vs. left).

This is why we came up with the name "Brothers Moving Forward" (B.M.F.) in thoughts, words, attitudes and actions. Since we believe that we fight from victory not for victory, we don't have anything to lose but everything to gain (in Heaven), also since the field is ripe to harvest in our very own backward, as America goes, so goes the rest of the world to a large degree. Let us remember the words of our Lord when He said, "He who puts his hand to the plow and looks back, is not fit for the kingdom of God." Brethren may we not disappoint!

After giving the matter much thought and prayer, we have decided to launch a full scale missionary expedition into the place where the greatest impact will be made to keep America civilized. This will be our first and primary missionary journey, and that is to go into the heart of the Leftist Black community. We believe that there is a substantial remnant of lost sheep in there who simply can't hear the shepherd's voice of truth because of all the noise, confusion and lies that the Libs have told.

It is obvious to see that although we are close geographically, we are as far apart spiritually as the east is from the west.

Brethren, to be blunt and perfectly honest, this is one missionary journey that you all should support as if the lives of you, your wife, sons, daughters and grandchildren depended on it. Because they very well might!

We could use all the physical, technical, and financial support you can spare, but most of all we need your prayers.

It would appear as though God has chosen Cleveland, Ohio to be ground zero, in that the nation has long since ridiculed and mocked this city as the "mistake on the lake," and now we also have the title of poorest major city in America. We all know how God loves to confound the wisdom of this world, and in James 2:5 God says that He "chose the poor to be rich in faith."

If we can make some traction here in Ohio, we will be looking to go national eventually. It all depends on if brothers moving forward in the Lord can make it happen.

From somewhere in the Deep Dark
Blue, your Brothers in Christ

# MY MINISTRY

Well folks, that's all I have for now.  Even though I could write for a 1,000 books, the spirit in me said I'm done for the time being. Most ministers want to be known as great men or women of God. They seek the reward of men, but me personally, if my work is a success, you will never know who I am.  My job is to give you some "face time" with Him.  After all, He is the one knocking at the door of your heart, asking you to let Him in to share with you and you with Him.  It is His love that has the power to save you if you will only believe.  So tap your brakes and slow yourself down to make sure you're on the right road, in the right direction.  He loves you more than you can imagine.  Do you love yourself?  The strong teach the weak, not vice versa.  Welcome to the real world!

I have told you the truth morally, ethically, philosophically, philanthropically, psychologically, chronologically, biblically, and theologically.  If you do not believe me, why not?  Please explain:

_____

_____

## BOOK SURVEY

This book was written for the two types of people in America and the world. They are the forward vs. backward, positive vs. negative, free vs. slave, strong vs. weak, right vs. left, intellectual vs. emotional, the saved vs. the unsaved. One group is happy and excited about the book, and the other group is apathetic and could care less.

**Question**: To which group do you belong and why?

**Explain**:

_____
_____
_____
_____
_____
_____
_____
_____
_____

# CONCLUSION

In conclusion, it is said, "A three fold cord is not easily broken."
Hence pride, apathy and selfishness are the cords that keep
mankind in bondage to sin. This discord keeps man at war with
God (pride), fellowman (apathy) and himself (selfishness).

The lion's share of any and all donations for this publication will
go towards making you and America whole, free and one—maybe
for the first time in your life and in this nation's history.

## *"Mable's Baby Boy"*

This book is in loving memory of and dedicated to Mable Bush, 2/24/37 to 9/7/07, from her "baby boy" Raymond Bush. Without her faith and love, this book would not have been possible.

Even in her death, she has given life to the "Burning Bush Ministry." If this book is able to help you to be free in this life and to find your salvation in the Lord and Savior Jesus Christ, then join with me in calling Mable Bush's life a true blessing to all that knew her. Amen.

www.ingramcontent.com/pod-product-compliance
Lightning Source LLC
Chambersburg PA
CBHW031248090426
42742CB00007B/360